RUBBING SHOULDERS

Karl Lagerfeld, Arlene Dahl, Marc Rosen

RUBBING SHOULDERS

MARC ROSEN

My Life with Popes, Princes,
Moguls, and Movie Stars

Foreword by Pamela Fiori

Glitterati
INCORPORATED
New York | London

ABOVE: CAROLE DELOUVRIER, MARC ROSEN, MICHAEL FEINSTEIN, TERRENCE FLANNERY, JOAN COLLINS, PERCY GIBSON

PREVIOUS PAGE: KARL LAGERFELD, ARLENE DAHL, MARC ROSEN

Dedication

To my wife, Arlene, whose beautiful shoulders have been
rubbing mine for over three decades.
My inspiration, my love.

To Pamela Fiori for suggesting
the title for this book. Thank you.

First published in 2016 by

Glitterati
INCORPORATED

New York | London

New York Office:
630 Ninth Avenue, Suite 603
New York, New York 10036
Telephone: 212 362 9119

London Office:
1 Rona Road
London NW3 2HY
Tel/Fax: +44 (0) 207 267 8339

www.GlitteratiIncorporated.com | media@GlitteratiIncorporated.com for inquiries

First edition, 2016

Library of Congress Cataloging-in-Publication data is available from the publisher.

Hardcover edition ISBN 13: 978-1-943876-01-3
Printed and bound in Canada
10 9 8 7 6 5 4 3 2 1

Photographs copyright © Peter Bacanovic at Doubles Club, pages 16 and 176

Marc Rosen, Liza Minnelli, Robert Osborne

MARC ROSEN, ARLENE DAHL

TABLE OF CONTENTS

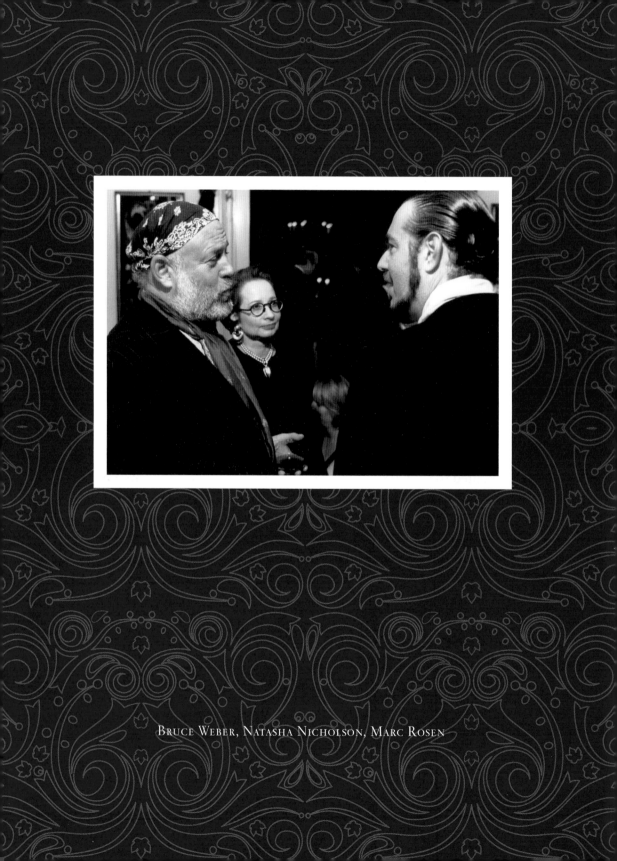

Bruce Weber, Natasha Nicholson, Marc Rosen

FOREWORD

Everybody's life is a story, but, let's face it some stories are more fascinating than others. It doesn't matter where you were born (to the manor or not), how or where you were raised, or under what circumstances. Nor does it make any difference whatsoever if you hail from royalty or abject poverty, from a white-collar or a blue-collar environment. What *does* matter is how you live, with whom you come into contact, what fortunes or misfortunes may occur, and how it all coalesces. I remember an article in *Esquire* years ago in which Norman Mailer, not exactly a modest man, interviewed himself. There was one exchange that has stuck with me to this day. Mailer's question: "What do you most regret in life?" Mailer's answer: "Every occasion I didn't rise to."

Marc Rosen, as you will soon learn, rose to almost every occasion presented to him. For a kid from New Jersey (I say this not with disdain but with admiration; I, too, am from the Garden State), Marc made the most of himself. Whether it had to do with a burning desire, creative talent, good luck, or all of the above, Marc was there (wherever "there" was) at the right time. And if it wasn't at the right time, it was usually when he was having a good time. There's no question that Marc is a man who savors life and lives in the moment, whether he's at a fancy dress ball or in the back of a taxi.

Mind you, he's rubbed shoulders with some incredibly high-profile people along the way, such as Pope John Paul II, Princess Grace of Monaco, and Imelda Marcos, to drop a few names. Indeed, Marc drops names with the same kind of nonchalance as that embodiment of urbanity, Noël Coward, and for exactly the same reason: he actually knew these people.

Marc credits me with suggesting the title of this book when we bumped into each other on the corner of Fifty-Ninth Street and Lexington Avenue some months ago. He told me he was writing a memoir about the famous characters he'd encountered in his lifetime. For some reason I blurted out, "Why don't you call it *Rubbing Shoulders?*" The words just tumbled forth. (Would that I could come up with a good title for one of my own books.)

Marc took the title and ran with it, using it as a motif for each personality he writes about. Padded Shoulders—Joan Crawford. Wet Shoulders—Esther Williams. Steinway Shoulders—Van Cliburn. Technicolor Shoulders—Arlene Dahl (the gorgeous actress who became his wife of thirty years). You get the idea.

The expression, of course, means coming into contact with powerful or celebrated people and receiving, as a result, some kind of social or psychic benefit. To rub shoulders with a president or prime minister, for instance, implies that your own standing has been elevated a notch or two.

Marc's anecdotes are delightful, surprising, sometimes shocking, and always told in a wry and witty way. If there were emoticons attached to each one, they would be some winking, laughing out loud, grimacing, grinning, and so on.

There are six chapters and forty-six sections in this book. That's a lot of brief encounters, but they make for a breezy and immensely enjoyable read. And at the end, they raise the question: "Who have *you* rubbed shoulders with lately?"

—Pamela Fiori

ANTHONY PERKINS, ELAINE STRITCH

MARC ROSEN

INTRODUCTION

When I was a child, my mother told me to stand straight to have good posture: "You have broad shoulders." Well, broad or not, they have been rubbing shoulders for over forty years with some of the most interesting people in the world.

My career in the cosmetics industry, along with my thirty-year marriage to film star Arlene Dahl, opened up a world to me filled with super-shoulders! Whether a pope, a princess, a pig, a taxi driver, an ambassador, a schnauzer, or a movie star, life is never boring.

Opportunity, happenstance, and serendipity have helped make the anecdotes in this book my reality. A few of the shoulders belong or belonged to: Julio Iglesias, Princess Grace of Monaco, Pope John Paul II, Imelda Marcos, Van Cliburn, Charles Revson, Tom Hanks, Lorenzo Lamas, Bette Davis, Olivia de Havilland, Joan Fontaine, Esther Williams, Karl Lagerfeld, the five Fendi sisters, Liza Minnelli, Joan Collins, Elsie de Wolfe, Joan Rivers, Michael Feinstein, Elaine Stritch, and, of course, my dear wife Arlene Dahl.

"Life is a banquet, and most poor suckers are starving to death," wrote Patrick Dennis in his novel *Auntie Mame*. It completely influenced my lifelong philosophy: be open to everything and amazing things can happen.

Rubbing Shoulders is a book that reminiscences over a life well spent. No regrets! I am still standing straight, Mother. Thank you for the good advice.

MARC ROSEN AS YOUNG BOY AGE 5

PROLOGUE

The people, places, and things that make up the anecdotes in this book are as real as my memory can recall and as elusive as a dream. I have spent my life in the pursuit of beauty, glamour, and the extraordinary. These stories are the amusing and poignant highlights. My earliest memory is bittersweet but certainly underscores my lifelong fascination with the special things life can offer.

When I was just three, I can vividly remember playing on our front lawn at dusk and hearing in the distance the jingling bells of what I hoped was the Good Humor ice cream truck arriving on our street. I ran into the house to ask my father for a dime to buy a Creamsicle. Instead it turned out to be a van selling balloons. Oh how I wanted one. I had never seen a balloon before, and I loved the way they floated in the air held by only a thin ribbon.

My father said I had to choose between ice cream or the balloon—a life lesson that I never learned. I wanted both! The balloon won out. Looking back now, I am astonished that even as a small child I chose a white balloon that I wanted tied to a white ribbon, as opposed to the rainbow of choices of brightly colored ones.

"Sonny, don't you want a red balloon?" the man offered.

"No, I want a white one," I stammered.

"Now hold on tight," my father said.

I proudly walked with him up toward the house, and then it happened: my little hand lost its grip and my beautiful white balloon floated up to the sky. My father tried to grab it, but it was too late. I cried and cried, but he said I should have listened. About a week later I looked out of my bedroom window at the night sky and saw the full moon. It's my balloon, I thought, up in the heavens for all to enjoy.

I still think of my elusive white bubble every time I look at the moon. Ain't life grand!

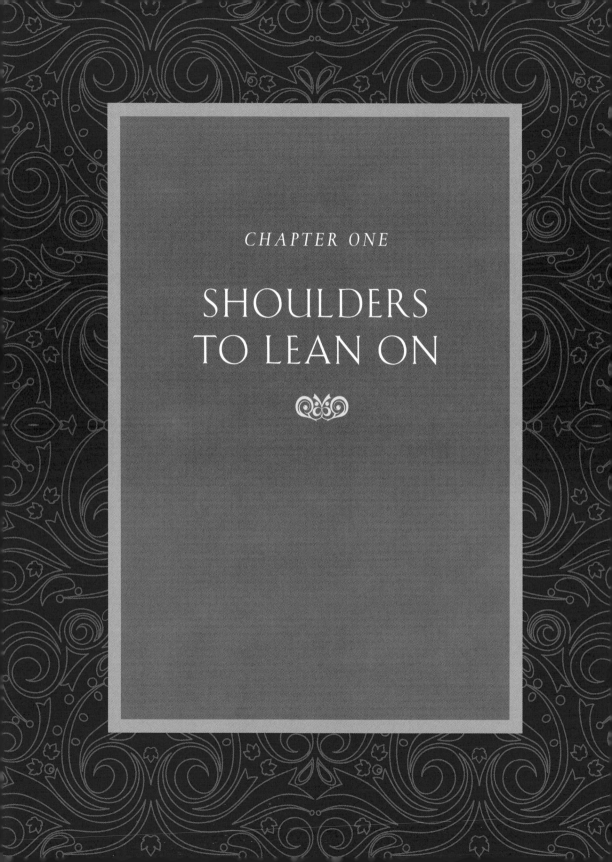

CHAPTER ONE

SHOULDERS TO LEAN ON

Antique Shoulders

When I was sixteen, I found God in Spring Valley, New York: my nirvana, the ultimate antique shop, right on Main Street. The proprietor, Norma Olin, was to become my mentor, my Auntie Mame.

She was a character right out of a Tennessee Williams play, a faded southern belle who fluttered around her cluttered, claustrophobic shop, overflowing with bric-a-brac, as if it were her antebellum ballroom. Mrs. Olin, as I always called her, was around sixty-five, ancient to a teenager. She wore false teeth but never had them in her mouth. She drawled through her gums, a nonstop monologue on antiques, southern humor, and her own brand of home-grown philosophy. She always wore pastel chiffon peignoirs and at least half a dozen art deco diamond bracelets up each arm, as well as rings on every finger.

I first met Spring Valley's answer to Blanche DuBois when I was out antique shopping with my parents. We tried to visit the Olin shop many times, but it was always closed. Finally, one lucky day, it appeared to be open. We rang the bell, and after what seemed like an endless wait through lights being turned on and strange shuffling noises, the door opened abruptly. It was kismet. There stood Norma Olin. I knew I had met my most unusual character, one whom *Reader's Digest* had not yet found out about.

Mrs. Olin loved the idea of a demented teenager who appreciated the Supremes and Chippendale at the same time. My thirst for knowledge was boundless, as was her enthusiasm for sharing it. We were the perfect "odd couple."

She taught me the difference between Sheraton and Hepplewhite, and I learned to distinguish the difference between Georgian and Victorian silver. Among Mrs. Olin's many charming eccentricities was her concept of the savings bank. It was a room-sized antique safe in the back room stuffed with cash, its drawers filled with silver dollars and vintage gold certificates. She didn't trust banks, never having gotten over the Depression.

Each year I would save my summer earnings to buy antiques—old Tiffany silver and Chinese export—items we chose together, which I still own and treasure. Mrs. Olin is long gone, but her spirit still glows in our dining room.

In a corner of the shop she had a narrow table covered with a linen runner, layers of dust, and various objets d'art. The table was the one piece she would never talk about. When I asked, she would always say, "We'll discuss that when you're older." Naturally, the table became my obsession.

Years later, when I married my first wife, I proudly drove her up to Spring Valley to meet Mrs. Olin, planning to select furniture for our first apartment—pieces with charm that hopefully we could afford.

Norma welcomed my wife into our special world and served us tea with her antique Limoges china. After a lovely visit, we chose a beautiful Empire mahogany dining table, a crystal chandelier, and silver candlesticks. As a wedding gift, Mrs. Olin gave us the table—I

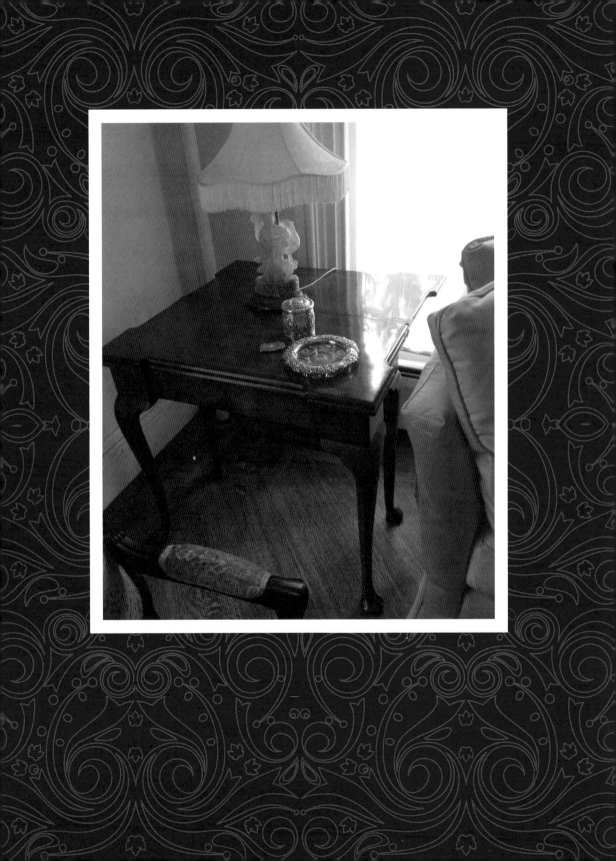

mean the mystery table. She had always been saving it for me, perhaps the son she never had. It was a rare eighteenth-century English card table that, I discovered later, was extremely valuable. She knew we would cherish it. It had found a good home.

Mrs. Olin told me the table was Queen Anne ... but for me it will always be Queen Norma.

Sophomore Shoulders

At the end of my freshman year at Carnegie Mellon University, dying to get out of the dorms, I had to choose between pledging a fraternity and getting my own apartment with a roommate. The choice was simple: an apartment.

Having walked back and forth many times from the campus to Shadyside, the artsy section of Pittsburgh, I had passed a series of wonderful old mansions built during the Gilded Age. When I found out that one of them rented apartments to CMU P&D (painting and design) and dramats (drama) students, I became obsessed with living there.

It was the limestone Gothic mansion standing on the corner of Amberson and Fifth Avenues. Built at the end of the nineteenth century by Willis McCook, a Scottish immigrant who became a Pittsburgh steel baron, to resemble a castle in his native land, it was home to me during my college years. Dominated by its matriarch, Margaret, the house and its mistress became an inseparable and remarkable force in my young life and has remained with me to this day. Set back from the street and surrounded by tall black wrought-iron gates, it seemed like the backdrop for Miss Havisham's salon in *Great Expectations*, and in a way it was.

An eclectic mix of architectural styles abounding with carved gargoyles, stained-glass windows, and fluted columns, it should have had a stately name like Dunleith or Wharton Hall to match the lofty facade, but instead it was simply known as Bonavita's, the family name of Margaret and Emil, the owners. How prophetic that a house known as Bonavita's, Latin for "good life," would have figured so prominently and indelibly in both my life and the lives of the countless other young people who lived there, many of whom went on to become famous in their fields.

On Christmas Eve 2003, Mrs. Bonavita (as I always called her) passed away at the age of ninety-two. Only a handful of people even noticed. Legends are made of celebrities who die in their prime, but long life seems to blur and even erase the achievements, as time sadly passes you by. Margaret Cecelia Joyce Holleran was born in Pittsburgh in 1912; an Irish lass, with all of the sass, spirit, and audacity of a Depression baby.

She used to tell me of how she would take the old trolley up Pittsburgh's Fifth Avenue and stare at the fabulous row of mansions still lining the avenue in Shadyside. In 1949, the Bonavitas were able to buy 5105 Fifth at a sheriff's sale for next to nothing. They restored the old house, which had been used for Army offices during World War II, with fluorescent lights jutting out of the elegant coffered ceilings into efficiency apartments.

Bonavita's soon become famous—or infamous—as the "artsy, bohemian" place to live if you were a painting and design or theater student. Not at all limited to CMU, the house attracted a wide range of, shall we say, "original" inhabitants. My roommate and I timidly walked through the gates and up the walk to the terrace surrounded by a carved balustrade topped with urns. We then made our way up to the double glass doors and peered into the enormous great hall, which culminated in a grand staircase with a

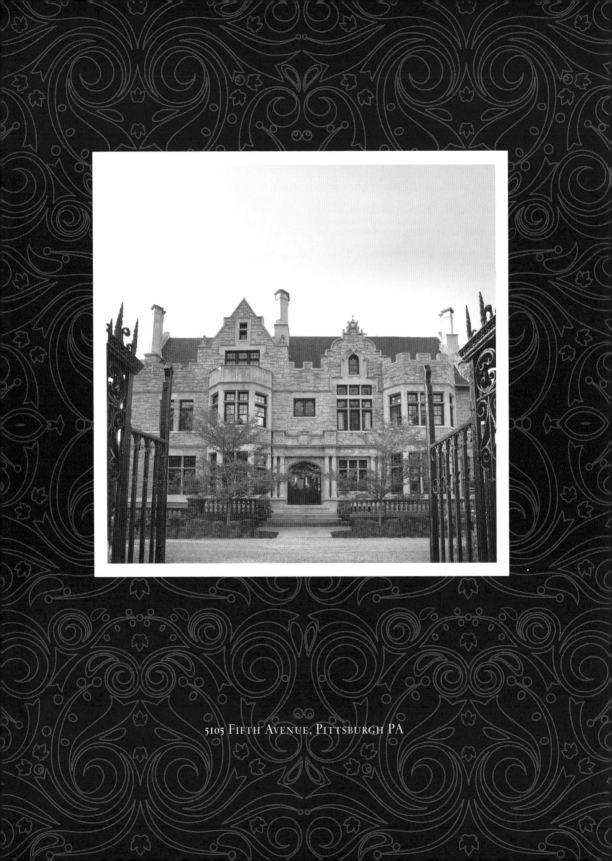

5105 Fifth Avenue, Pittsburgh PA

two-story stained-glass nave at the first landing. Merchant Ivory, eat your hearts out.

After ringing the bell with great trepidation, we waited an inordinate time until a strange woman right out of central casting for the part of Mrs. Quasimodo answered the door. I knew we weren't in Kansas anymore. We were ushered into a large salon with a twenty-foot white rococo ceiling that must have been concocted by a pastry chef. There amidst the shabby genteel antique decor sat Mrs. Bonavita herself, sprawled atop a black leather Barcalounger with her leg extended and bandaged, suffering from a case of phlebitis. In a shabby housedress and with ruddy Irish cheeks, she seemed more the maid than the mistress of the manse. What a lesson I was to learn about not judging a book by its proverbial cover. I didn't know it at that moment, but she was to become my second mother and certainly my most unforgettable character.

My life had just changed, and my new education by exposure would rival the one at CMU for its influence on me. It was a three-year life experience I will never forget. I became her "adopted son" and was given the premier suite, made up from what had been the old master bedroom, which I decorated with antique furniture swiped from the other apartments during the summer. She took me to auctions and I learned about antiques, building on what I knew by visiting Norma Olin, and it became a lifetime passion. She even let me bid for her so the dealers in the room wouldn't bid against her.

I had bashes in the billiard room, and we drove to Harrisburg to see her friend, Governor David Lawrence—mighty heady stuff. After telling an unwanted tenant on the floor below that the house was haunted by the ghost of Mr. McCook's mad cousin, who supposedly was chained in the attic, we dragged chains on the floor of the attic to scare him out.

Along with choosing package design as my career direction, appreciating the beauty and spirituality of the past, and going "all the way" with my girlfriend, Bonavita's was my "coming of age" experience. I was but one of the many whose lives were touched by knowing this great lady.

Her son Charles tells me I was the only one of them who stayed in touch. Of this I am proud.

Last night I dreamt that I went back to 5105 Fifth to see Mrs. Bonavita, but she's no longer at home—she is in residence in my heart.

GLASS SHOULDERS—
HOTEL SPLENDIDO, PORTOFINO

For over twenty-five years I have been fortunate enough to be invited to Monaco to create a panel of experts at Luxe Pack Monaco, the luxury cosmetics packaging show. Most people go to places like Cincinnati on business trips, but when you're in the beauty business, you go to Monte Carlo. I invited Kevin Marshall, my longtime colleague at the time. As we wanted to take a day trip, I suggested Portofino, a spot I had enjoyed years before. He had never been there, and I thought it would be fun introducing him to the beautiful Italian seaside village.

It was the end of October, and although the "season" was over—and it was raining to boot—we ventured out undaunted. Donning trench coats and umbrellas, we were on our way. The concierge had misled us into thinking it was an hour-and-a-half drive, but with the rain slowing us down, it took us almost three hours. We were tired and hungry. The village looked quiet with all of the tourists gone. We drove around looking for a nice place to have lunch. Finally, looming large was a billboard for the Hotel Splendido, famous for film star trysts in the fifties. Perfect! Driving in the fog we saw it on a cliff looking over a private cove, almost eerie in that light.

By the time we arrived at the hotel, I could have eaten the menu. Wearing my raincoat, I walked toward the table. Kevin had gone to the restroom. There was a long counter covered with stemmed wineglasses stacked in tiers. I removed my coat to place it on the chair and heard what sounded like a distant crash of glass. It seemed to go on for minutes and was quite alarming in its intensity. As I sat down, the people at the surrounding tables looked at me askance. *Why*, I thought. Then it dawned on me: I had created the great crash by hitting the glasses with my trench coat. Oh my God, I was in shock. I had caused this gigantic waste of over a hundred glasses. I was a destructive, terrible person.

Rejoining me at the table, Kevin witnessed the mess and asked what had happened. He had heard the crash all the way on the floor below. "We will have to wash dishes for a month to pay for this," I murmured. The maître d' came over and I apologized profusely. He shrugged, smiled, and said, "*Nessun problema, sono solo bicchieri di vino!*" No problem, they're only wine glasses. "What would you like to order for lunch?" Kevin and I looked at each other and realized that glasses could be replaced. Life was more about the view of the lagoon, the ambience, and good food than shattered glass. Think Italian!

Rubbing Shoulders at the Hôtel du Cap

As Arlene's sixth husband—count them, six—I take heart in the fact that I have by far lasted the longest. Her fourth husband was French wine entrepreneur Alexis Lichine. A marketing genius, he is credited with making French wine popular in America. They were married for five years, and along with her two eldest children, Carole and Lorenzo, Arlene summered at his chateaux in Bordeaux along with his two children, Sacha and Alexandra.

Fade out. In 1986 Alexis had gone on to his great reward. Arlene, stepmother extraordinaire, maintained a wonderful relationship with both children. Sacha inherited the chateau, modernized the winery, and was a great guy in his early thirties spending holidays in Saint-Tropez. That August we were invited to be houseguests at a friend's place in the south of France and called Sacha to say we were there and hoped to see him. He had rented a villa and had houseguests but wanted to invite us to meet them for lunch at the Hôtel du Cap.

Sacha and Co. had arrived across the bay via his motorboat. We had great fun catching up and laughing about growing up "Lichine." I was sitting next to Sacha's lady friend. After a few glasses of rosé, confided that when Sacha had woken them up that morning he announced that instead of having another laid-back day on the beach, they would be going to the hotel to meet his stepmother and her husband for lunch and had to "dress up."

"Arlene," he said with great fondness, "will be dressed in a wonderful designer dress wearing a hat and dark glasses."

"Don't be silly," she told him. "We're in the south of France. Nobody dresses that way."

"Arlene will," he replied, still imagining her as she looked when he first met her.

When they arrived, she was flabbergasted that Arlene looked exactly as Sacha had remembered her. Dressed in her best movie star garb—black-and-white printed frock, huge black straw hat, and dark glasses—it looked like she had just stepped off of a film set. My wife never disappoints.

STEP SHOULDERS

I have three wonderful stepchildren thanks to Arlene and three of her earlier marriages. Over the last decades we have had many great experiences together. Here are three of them.

CAROLE'S GRADUATION

Arlene's daughter, Carole, is a terrific and beautiful gal. In the late seventies, when she was graduating from the very tony Miss Porter's School, we went up to Connecticut for the outdoor ceremony. It was a warm, beautiful day in June. We drove up from the city and were running late. Arlene was wearing a pale gray silk dress, gray kid gloves, and a silver-gray fox boa. I was in a white suit and pastel tie—very garden party. In Hollywood, that is. We would have been perfect in the opening scene of *The Great Gatsby*. But this was WASP heaven; little print shifts from Lilly Pulitzer were the uniform for moms, and navy blazers, tan slacks with embroidered boats or frogs, and rep ties were for dads. To say that we misjudged the situation was an understatement. Carole nearly died. To boot, her father, Chris Holmes, was there with his arm in a sling and three sheets to the wind.

The graduating young women, all in white and united by holding a garland of white flowers, looked like vestal virgins out for their last gig. After the ceremony, which seemed endless in the ninety-degree heat, we met Carole in an open field. She and her friends were crying, hugging each other and saying their heartfelt goodbyes.

Marc Rosen, Carole Delouvrier

That night was the big prom. Getting a date was the challenge. Arlene came through by asking her dear friend, Mary Roebling, the first female bank president in America and the daughter-in-law of the man who built the Brooklyn Bridge, to ask her godson, Thomas Flagg, to escort Carole. As I waited for this farewell lovefest to end, a large black limo pulled up. The chauffer opened the passenger door and a plump, rather stiff young man appeared. He asked me which one of these gals was Carole Holmes. I introduced myself as her stepfather and pointed her out. He had one of those lockjaw boarding school accents I found very amusing. Trying to make conversation, I asked him where he was from.

He replied, "The Gaaaden Staaate."

"Where?" I asked.

"Oh," he paused, "we don't like to say New Jersey."

Poor Carole!

STEPHEN, PLACE DES VOSGES

My stepson Stephen is a talented sculptor who, at age eighteen, was backpacking through Europe, staying at youth hostels, crashing at a convent in Venice and on the balcony of Paris's Shakespeare and Company bookstore, and sleeping on uncomfortable seats on second-class railways cars. Ah, to be young! As I was coming to Paris on business, I suggested that he meet me to finally have a good night's sleep in a real bed.

I was staying at the Bristol. I arrived from the airport very jet-lagged and fell asleep. I told the desk to send him up to my room when he arrived. Stephen must have enjoyed the fine French linens and cozy comforter, because he was fast asleep when I came out of my coma. I had made dinner reservations at a very good restaurant called Coconnas, located under the eighteenth-century arches of the Place des Vosges. It would be his first square meal in months, in style!

At the table, I was still very tired and struggling to stay awake. Stephen was young and impressionable. The service was terrible. We waited for what seemed like half an hour before the waiter came by. Very French and arrogant, he sized us up as "*Américains.*" I ordered white wine in my best restaurant French. He repeated *vin blanc* as a question to make me feel that my pronunciation was imperfect. I was not intimidated, but Stephen was embarrassed. I was getting rather irritated, as I wanted to order and the menus never arrived. Every attempt to get the waiter's attention failed. He was always looking the other way. Finally he appeared with the menus and we ordered. Half an hour went by and the cold starters had not arrived. I miraculously caught his eye and asked where the appetizers were. He imperiously said, "If you are in a rush, you can go down the street for a *croque* and a Coke." That's just what we did!

Flying Down to Key West— Lorenzo Lamas

My stepson Lorenzo Lamas is a well-known TV actor. He loves women, children, and speed, in that order—with five wives and six children to prove it. He enjoys the thrill of living on the edge. On a TV show called *Celebrity Daredevils*, he once jumped a motorcycle off an eighty-five-foot ramp in the rain over thirteen Chrysler PT Cruisers—not for the faint of heart. He has flown and owned his own plane and raced Formula One cars in professional meets.

Lorenzo is a terrific guy, and we are very close. Perhaps after having four stepfathers he decided I was a keeper.

Several years ago, he and his family were visiting us at our home in Palm Beach. His wife, number four, a former *Playboy* centerfold, and their three little girls flew there commercial while Lorenzo flew his new plane, a Piper Seneca Cub two-seater, solo from Los Angeles. He suggested that it would be fun for the two of us to take a trip to Key West for lunch the next day. I agreed. *Why not?* Why not…. Me, whose idea of risk was taking Air France first class with a Valium. Me, whose idea of skiing was only *après*! Was I nervous about flying over miles of the Everglades with nothing but swamps and alligators below? Did I trust a man who would drive a motorcycle over a Mack truck? Maybe. After all, he was alive to tell the tales.

The next day we set off for the airport. His plane was *small*! Somehow "size mattered." This was like a toy, but what did I know? I must say I was impressed with his amazing attention to details. He

Marc Rosen, Lorenzo Lamas

checked and rechecked every gadget on the plane, except the gas.... Once we got up in the air he casually mentioned that he thought we had just enough fuel to get us to Key West but would have to get gas for the return trip. Sounded reasonable. I decided to sit back and enjoy the experience and the scenery. Let go and let God! It was a beautiful trip, and Lorenzo was a very capable and serious pilot.

We landed smoothly and took a taxi to enjoy lunch at a restaurant he said was very famous. Blue Heaven, which served Caribbean specialties including fried conch, had been around for decades. Not my favorite, with steel drums beating nonstop and live chickens clucking and pecking the earth under our table as we ate. This was not what I expected heaven to be like, blue or otherwise. Key West was supposed to be an island with white Victorian cottages and swaying palms. This was the home of Somerset Maugham and other noted writers who drank rum and did decadent things too tawdry to repeat.

I had another mai tai and enjoyed Lorenzo's company.

When we got to the airport for our return, Lorenzo planned to refuel. He thought I didn't notice the guy shake his head *no* as in "out of fuel." He told me he thought it would be fun to stop at another island en route. My ears were still ringing from the beat of the steel drums, and I was done in after a few drinks, but I wanted to be a good sport. Marco Island was no more than a dirt runway, but it did have a gas pump. I knew that he was breathing a sigh of relief and, frankly, so was I!

Rubbing Maxi's Shoulders—
Our Schnauzer

Maxi was all black with a white beard and chest. He was so handsome and well behaved that everywhere we walked people would stop to tell me what a looker he was. I was like chopped liver. On the day of New Year's Eve a few years ago, I was walking him into an outdoor café in Palm Beach to have breakfast. We passed our dear friend Nancy Tsai eating with her pal, Nancy Brinker, the founder of the Susan G. Komen Breast Cancer Foundation and former ambassador to Hungary. Divorced and very attractive, she took one look at Maxi and asked if he could be her date that night, as he was already in black tie!

Liza's Shoulders

Liza has been a close friend for many years. We attended her infamous wedding to David Gest. Arlene had known her since she was a child, having been good friends with her famous parents.

We both had miniature schnauzers. Arlene and I had Maxi (or Maximillian), and Liza had Emelina. One day the phone rang and it was Liza.

"Honey, do you want to mate the kids?" Emelina was going into heat any day.

Arlene and I thought, *why not*! Emelina and Liza had all the work and Maxi all the fun. A few days later, Liza called to say I should

Arlene Dahl, Liza Minnelli

bring Maxi over to her apartment the next morning. She was so into it I couldn't believe it. She had breeders and vets on call.

When I arrived at eight o'clock in the morning with Maxi in tow, I expected the housekeeper to answer the door. Wrong—it was Liza, who normally slept until noon, very excited about the task ahead. We introduced the dogs, and I departed. I said I would come to walk Maxi at noon and hoped "the deed" would be done.

Returning later, I asked Liza how it was going.

"Well, honey, they are just crazy about each other, but they don't seem to know which end needs attention."

I took my little boy for a walk and had a father-son talk with him: "Humping Emelina's face may be a lot of fun, but it won't produce any babies. You need to hump her other end!"

I brought him back to the loving paws of Emy and told Liza I had given Max my fatherly wisdom and would call later.

When I telephoned at three o'clock, a very happy Ms. Minnelli told me that they had "done it" two times. I guess Maxi heard me! Emelina had four pups, and we were very proud grandparents.

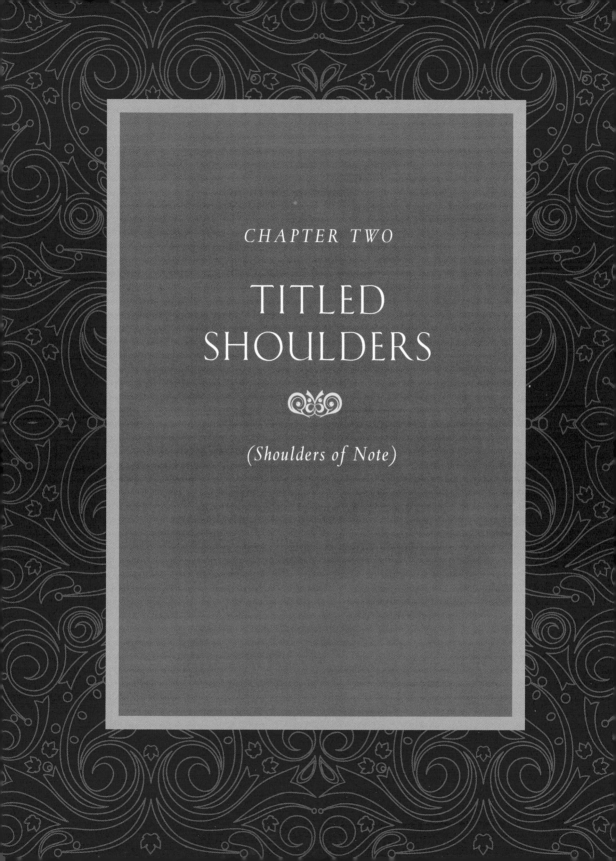

CHAPTER TWO

TITLED
SHOULDERS

(Shoulders of Note)

Papal Shoulders— Pope John Paul II

In the halcyon days of the early eighties, cosmetic companies making European designer fragrances felt they should support their licensees by sending their creative and marketing teams to attend fashion designers' fall and spring collections for inspiration. While at Elizabeth Arden, I was privileged to join my colleagues for these very glamorous trips to Paris for a week of dinners, meetings, the collections, and fun. As we were working with both the House of Chloé and Karl Lagerfeld, and later with Fendi, it was exciting to say the least.

I was in my early thirties and single again after an earlier marriage. The show began on a Monday, so I decided I would fly to Rome the Friday before to shop on Via Condotti, their Madison Avenue, for ideas, and maybe for a new suit for the next morning. The shops closed at 1:00 p.m. I was unaware that Sunday would be the investiture of a new pope at the Vatican. He was to be called Pope John Paul II. There was wild anticipation since he was the first non-Italian pope in over four hundred years, and would be the first Polish pope. This came on the heels of the mysterious demise of the man chosen to be pope only a short time earlier.

After arriving at the Hotel Hassler, located at the top of the Spanish Steps, I decided to take a walk and ran into a friend from New York who was an important ecclesiastical publisher. He told me he was there for the big event, as Rome was packed with cardinals, bishops, and priests. He invited me to dinner that night, asking if I minded being the token Jew, as his guests were all men of the cloth. I reminded him that Christ was Jewish and promptly accepted. We were going to a fashionable new restaurant on Piazza del Popolo called Il Bolognese. Sounded good to me.

When I arrived, the holy group was already feeling no pain. After a few glasses of wine we became kindred spirits. They inquired what I did for a living, and I said that, like them, I was in the business of religion—the religion of beauty. They loved it. At one point late in the evening, someone asked me if I would like to join them in the morning to attend the pope's first international press event. No one had laid eyes on him yet. I was embarrassed to say I was planning to go shopping, my real reason for visiting Rome. I assumed the press event would be a madhouse with thousands of people and that I would never get close enough to see the pope.

They asked if I had a photo for them to create a press badge, and I said no, thinking this would be the end of it. But it was not to be. He suggested that our merry group go to the train station to have me shot in one of those old-fashioned photo booths. Off we went, and the machine spit out three little pictures. I was off to see the wizard—I mean the pope! The die was cast, and I would meet the group at Saint Peter's Basilica in the morning. Via Condotti would have to wait.

The next morning, I joined this distinguished group at the entrance to the right colonnade of Saint Peter's. I started to feel less anxious when I laid eyes on the pageantry of the Swiss guards overseeing the immense doors: spears, helmets, and all regalia in place. We climbed a hundred stone steps only to face another pair of Swiss guards. I was enjoying this, all very historic and grand. This was a private entrance to the Vatican that mere mortals never witnessed—more steps, more guards. When we reached the *primo piano* we walked through endless art galleries filled with huge tapestries, carved chests, and religious paintings that made the Cloisters in New York seem shabby. My head was on a swivel, realizing this was an incredible experience—much better than shopping.

We finally reached the large room where the pope was to appear. Vaulted ceilings, pews to seat only a hundred people, and in the front of the chamber, a raised platform holding a gilded throne—so far, so good. I took my place on the aisle amidst a flurry of photographers hoping to get the first picture of the Polish pope. The entrance to the twenty-foot-ceilinged salon was draped in purple velvet, very papal.

When in Italy, because of my slicked-back hair, beard, and Mediterranean complexion, people assumed I was Italian. Loving the country passionately, I was able to speak Italian phrases with a decent accent mixed with appropriate enthusiasm and enough gestures to pass for a native. This proved to be a plus.

The room went silent, a solemn moment. Then the drapes parted, and there, flanked by cardinals in crimson, was Pope John Paul II, all in white—a vision to be sure. His blue eyes were compelling. As he slowly made his way down the aisle, I became transfixed. He stopped at my pew halfway down and looked at me. Having an out-of-body experience, I stammered "*Santo Padre*." He touched my shoulder. The pope touched me! As if that weren't enough, he stood on the platform and spoke to the audience in Italian, making the gestures of a blessing. I asked the photographer next to me what he had said.

"The pope has given us a papal dispensation, absolving us of all of our sins to date."

Well, I was ready to convert! Now I could start sinning with a clean plate!

A Baron's Shoulders—
Kasteel de Haar

My dear stepdaughter Carole, in between marriages, was seriously dating a charming older gentleman named Teddy van Zuylen, who happened to be a Dutch baron. His ancestral home was Kasteel de Haar, the largest castle in Holland. We liked him very much, and having a castle wasn't bad either. He would visit Carole in New York every few months, and we would always enjoy having dinner with him. His little gifts to Carole from Cartier were endearing to say the least. Carole would often meet him in London or Paris and was invited with her small children to stay at the castle. Since Arlene and I, as Americans, didn't have many or any close friends who happened to own their own castle, we were anxious to hear all about it when she returned.

"Well, how was it?" I asked.

"Oh, it was nice," was her only reply.

We assumed that maybe it was "shabby genteel," and she was being polite.

A few months later Teddy told us that once a year he brings in a great French chef and invites a small group of friends to stay for a week, and he asked us to come. We thought this meant an engagement announcement was imminent, and accepted. We flew to Amsterdam and spent the night. The next morning Teddy sent a car to fetch us. Riding on the highway, I noticed an exit sign for "de Haar." How interesting, I thought, the castle and the village have the same name. Little did I know the village was erected by Teddy's ancestors for the workmen and craftsmen who had built the castle.

We got off at the exit and there, looming large, was an enormous castle à la the famous Disneyland one. Behold, the turrets were topped with red pennants that matched the red shutters. As we drove up to the drawbridge—yes, a drawbridge—I thought, "Wow, this is the real deal!" We proceeded onto the estate, and I noticed a large stone stable on the left, a maze (you don't see many mazes these days) on the right, and finally, another drawbridge over the moat, in which two black swans were floating. Finally, as we approached the enormous staircase leading to the castle's entrance, I spotted Carole and Teddy walking down to meet us. When I could catch Carole alone, I whispered, "Nice." Is that the only word you could use to describe this place?

Later, after taking a bicycle ride around the grounds, I admired the church—they have their own church—deer preserve, and a gardener's cottage, a perfect retirement home for the in-laws.

When I got back to our suite, I was so excited that I called our friend Joan Rivers to share our news. After relating the details I have just offered, she said, "Are you kidding, Carole should marry him just for the stationery!"

Rubbing Shoulders with
the Romanovs

While at Elizabeth Arden from 1978 to 1988, I created a series of annual holiday porcelain collections based upon great palaces of the world, each to be filled with bath powders, soap, and the like. Working with the museum directors, I would bring a photographer and my design assistant to the venue to be inspired to create the pieces. We'd had great success with collections based on the Royal Pavilion at Brighton in England, the Palace of Versailles, the Topkapi Palace in Istanbul, and so on. My dream was to do the grand palaces in Leningrad, before and now known again as Saint Petersburg. Studying the dramatic history of that time and the tragic end of the Russian royal family was a great pastime of mine. This was in the early eighties, and the Cold War was still very much in effect. I had recently picked up a copy of Robert K. Massie's best-selling historical biography, *Nicholas and Alexandra*, chronicling the rise and fall of the Romanov dynasty, and I was absorbed in every detail.

The Alexander Palace, outside of the city in Tsarskoye Selo, was the family's favorite residence. There they lived in privacy with their four daughters and son. Their legendary collection of Fabergé eggs, the czarina's mauve boudoir, the malachite and vermeil urns, and the Russian icons were all a designer's dream.

I longed to have this palace for my next collection. The president of Arden approved it. Now all I needed was to figure out how to get past the protocol and bureaucracy of the Soviet State. I found out from the Russian consulate in New York that their minister of culture would be coming to the city. I wrote explaining what we had done with past collections, working with other countries, and asked to meet with him in New York. To my amazement and joy, he responded and agreed to meet me for lunch. I took him to an authentic Russian restaurant in Manhattan's Lower East Side. Over borscht and pierogies I got him to agree to allow us to "officially" create the collection. His office would make all of the arrangements.

Traveling with photographer and friend Peter Millard and my colleague designer Lannie Hart, I arrived by Aeroflot, the official Soviet airline. We were driven to the venerable Hotel Astoria, a grand nineteenth-century building that had lost its luster fifty years before. Not to be disillusioned, I was bound and determined to enjoy this step back in time. The Soviet regime had no respect for anything from before 1917. The great palaces were now multiple-family dwellings or government institutions. The broad boulevards had no automobiles driving on them. The store windows featured displays of canned food arranged in pyramids. Queues of people waited outside shops. The color was gray, everywhere gray.

We were not allowed to venture outside the hotel unchaperoned. Our itinerary was prearranged by the minister's office and would begin in the morning. I was shown to an enormous suite crowded with bulky grim velvet, upholstered couches and chairs, and huge, dark wooden armoires. The foyer featured a huge white refrigerator, and the tap water ran brown and smelled—so far, so good…

The next morning, I went down to the dining room with my colleagues expecting a hearty Russian breakfast complete with delicious black pumpernickel bread. The buffet was served by large, bulky women wearing white uniforms and hairnets, ladling out a thick cereal that looked like gruel. Not a pretty way to start the day. Afterwards we went to the front desk to inquire about our tour. We were told that everything was closed for a national holiday. And so it went.

Finally we were told we would be going to Tsarskoye Selo to see the great palace built by Catherine the Great. When we arrived, I told the guide we would be designing a porcelain collection, and she directed us to follow her to a very large, musty room with a twenty-foot ceiling, carved paneling, and a parquet floor that went beyond shabby genteel.

The floors were covered with stacks of antique porcelain—fabulous pieces that should have been catalogued and placed in a showcase. I was on my knees, savoring these treasures of a bygone era, when I looked up and saw the walls had been upholstered in mauve silk brocade, now faded and in tatters. Of the hundreds of rooms in this enormous palace, fate had landed me in Alexandra's famous mauve boudoir, the scene of the many encounters I had just read about in Massie's new book. The room where the royal family would meet for tea with the children. The dramatic scenes with the Dowager Empress and Alexandra and her bizarre encounters with Rasputin. This was her most personal refuge from the court that hated her so. A chill ran through me. Happenstance again had prevailed.

Rubbing Royal Shoulders—
Princess Grace of Monaco

Both Arlene and Grace Kelly had been under contract to MGM, and they remained friends long after she married Prince Rainier of Monaco. During our courtship and marriage we often vacationed and would see the princess for tea or cocktails. One summer we had been invited by John Mills and his new wife to cruise on their yacht. John was London's famous impresario and owned the illustrious gambling club Les Ambassadeurs.

We arrived in Monte Carlo and checked into the Hôtel de Paris, as we were to board the boat in the morning. The yacht, however, needed repairs, and as our trip would be delayed by a few days we were to be John's guests at the hotel in the interim.

The next day, Grace invited us to the palace for drinks. She asked Arlene if she could host their annual Red Cross Ball that Saturday night. It was their most glamorous event of the year. Arlene was very flattered but explained that we were due to leave the next day on John Mills's yacht. As it turned out, the boat's repairs would take longer than expected, or rather it was a "princess's prerogative." Grace had pulled a favor, and Arlene would be her "host with the most."

The palace sent a huge black vintage Rolls to fetch us, and we were off to the ball. Arlene made a beautiful and charming host, and I was so proud of her. During cocktails, the guests were atwitter with excitement over the evening's entertainer, who was already a big name in Europe but as yet unknown in the United States. When Arlene introduced the Latin singing sensation, the elegant, tiara-topped, couture-clad women in the audience threw caution to the wind and carried on like teenaged girls. I thought he was smarmy and obvious as the Latin lover crooner with his whispery, sexy voice.

"He'll never make it in the States," I sneered. His name was Julio Iglesias. Guess I was wrong.

Princess Grace of Monaco— Second Story

Having met Princess Grace many times in Monaco, New York, and even her hometown of Philadelphia, I came upon the idea of asking her to collaborate with me on the creation of a porcelain collection based on Monaco. I had noticed there was nothing for a tourist to purchase as a memento there, other than a white china plate with badly drawn profiles of the prince and princess. I knew how to design and have annual porcelain collections produced, and this would be something I would take on myself.

When I approached Grace with the idea, she loved it, and was especially delighted because there was a porcelain factory in Monaco that could produce it. She was bursting with ideas based upon the botanical and Japanese gardens she had helped create, their famous aquarium, and naturally her beautiful pink palace. We began working in earnest. She was a pleasure to work with and loved my sketches. We met several times in the large Park Avenue apartment of fashion designer Vera Maxwell, where she stayed when coming alone.

As we needed to put together the business aspect, I was told to contact a gentleman who was the head of the Société des Bain de Mer, which the prince headed and controlled all of the hotels, casinos, and clubs. While on a business trip we made a date to meet at the townhouse where the royal family lived when in Paris, on a cul-de-sac off the exclusive Avenue Foch.

Grace welcomed me graciously but nervously, and after introducing me to the executive, she left us alone. It was awkward but became even more so when the executive confided that the prince was "not amused" and, in fact, did not want the princess engaged in commercial projects. I tried to explain how this would promote tourism and create jobs, but it was to no avail. He was unpleasant and dismissive. I sadly realized the trade-off Grace Kelly had made to become a princess. I hoped it was worth it.

THE KAISER'S SHOULDERS

During my time at Arden, I also worked with Karl Lagerfeld, designing his fragrance bottles, where they had the license for Chloé and Lagerfeld fragrances.

It was always a very creative experience, with Karl dropping *bons mots* as directions. When I designed his famous "KL" perfume collection as a fan-shaped bottle, he saw it and proclaimed, "I am a fan of fans."

It all began with one of his unique phone calls: "Hello, it's Karl. I am calling you from Versailles, where I just saw the Concorde flying over Le Petit Trianon. Imagine, the best of the twentieth century and the best of the eighteenth century colliding. This could inspire you, Marc!"

I hung up, staring out of my Manhattan office building, looking at another across the street, and trying desperately to imagine the scene he had just described. What to do?

I began by trying to conjure up some element from the eighteenth century that had meaning in our time. I seized upon the fan, a fashion accessory of the time that was now used only in the context of a costume party. I did research; contrary to my belief that *Gone with The Wind* fans were used to ventilate hot and bothered southern belles glistening on verandas of great plantations, they were actually "weapons of flirtation," and that flirtation doubtless included a fragrance wafting about a young lovely.

A perfect symbol for Karl's fragrance, as he is known for carrying fans himself as a fashion accessory. Inspiration comes from odd places. Thank you, Karl.

Marc Rosen, Arlene Dahl

Rubbing Shoulders on the
High Seas—Our Elopement

When Arlene and I became engaged in 1981, it caused quite a kerfuffle. In those days women simply did not marry much younger men. Arlene was a cougar before the word became part of the vernacular. Just one example was the outraged president of Elizabeth Arden, who came into my office one day waving a copy of the *National Enquirer*, announcing that Arlene Dahl was engaged to an Elizabeth Arden executive eighteen years her junior. I reminded him that his lovely wife happened to be sixteen years younger than he was.

People who had known Arlene through her five previous marriages were skeptical about our future. "It will never last" was the general consensus. Well, they were wrong. We just celebrated our thirtieth anniversary.

After a prolonged engagement, we decided to elope on the first small luxury cruise ship, *The Sea Goddess*. We boarded the ship in Marbella and debarked in Monte Carlo. In Marbella we were feted at the Marbella Club by the owner, Alfonso von Hohenlohe, and at a charming luncheon hosted by Avon heiress Terry von Pantz. The wedding party was attended by 007 star Sean Connery and his wife, Micheline, and actress Linda Christian, once married to Tyrone Power, among others. When we arrived in Monaco, our friend, Countess Donina Cicogna, hosted a luncheon onboard.

One of the guests was the Princess Bismarck, an older German aristocrat. Arlene and I were seated at different tables, and the princess asked Arlene to point out her new husband. She gestured over to me.

"What is his name?"

"Marc Rosen," Arlene replied.

"Oh, the von Rooosens," she exclaimed. "They are a noble Swedish family. How nice for you, my dear."

To this day I pull out my "von" with an imaginary monocle when I want a laugh.

CHAPTER THREE

RUBBING WITH THE RARIFIED

Padded Shoulders— Joan Crawford

Our first night on a cruise ship sailing the Caribbean, Arlene and I met a woman named Beatrice who was a professional psychic and clairvoyant. My wife, my favorite astrologer, is also clairvoyant. By kismet, we became chummy, as you tend to do on these voyages. We soon developed a small group who were all interested in having the psychic conduct a séance.

The next evening after dinner we gathered in our stateroom, prepared to delve into the beyond! We gathered on chairs surrounding the facilitator, with Arlene perched on a stool. Several of the people asked Beatrice to try to connect with friends or family members "on the other side." After three or four of these souls reached out to their loved ones, we all started to relax and get into the spirit of it—pardon the pun! Like a scene from a B-movie, it began thundering and the boat hit turbulence, rocking us around the room. Suddenly Arlene was thrown off of the stool and the skin around the psychic's neck was turning red.

She was struggling to speak. Who was trying to come through? Someone's sainted mother? A murdered soul trying to reach out for justice? No, of all the possible dearly departed it was Joan Crawford, recently exploited to a fare-thee-well in the book *Mommy Dearest*, penned by her vitriolic, adopted daughter Christina. The book had been a sensation, completely vilifying Joan, who had been a great film star and personality. Wire coat hangers became the butt of many jokes. Arlene had known Joan both negatively and positively over the years. Now she was speaking through the psychic, begging Arlene to help set the record straight by denying these heinous charges.

What a shock! After Joan said her piece, we the audience hoped this strong force would return to Hollywood heaven. It was not to be. So strong was her aura that the psychic had to exorcise the suite to remove her presence.

Rubbing Elsie's Shoulders

When Arlene arrived in Hollywood, she was fortunate enough to meet Elsie and Sir Charles Mendl. Elsie was, of course, the famous decorator who had practically invented the profession, and also Hollywood's leading hostess. She is still revered as one of the greatest interior designers of her time. Elsie and Charles practically adopted Arlene in Hollywood; they invited her to all their parties and later to stay with them at Elsie's home in Versailles, the Villa Trianon. This was where Elsie had entertained the likes of Jean Cocteau, Elsa Schiaparelli, Mona Bismarck, Cole and Linda Porter, Coco Chanel, and the Duke and Duchess of Windsor.

Just before we were to be married in 1980, a biography of Elsie was published. I enjoyed reading it, knowing of Arlene's history with her. The great house had been traded by Elsie, always the shrewd business woman, to Paul-Louis Weiller, known as the Commandant. Enormously rich, the founder of Air France, he had singlehandedly saved the French economy during World War I. Weiller, a collector and savior of many great French chateaux, had agreed to trade her the villa for life occupancy and a string of perfect pearls. As she was already in her late eighties at the time, it seemed like a good bargain. Elsie of course fooled him by living another eight years.

Arlene and I flew to Paris en route to Marbella for our honeymoon. Our friend Maggi Nolan, the owner of Paris's Celebrity Service, hosted a luncheon for us at her club. Olivia de Havilland, her daughter Gisele, and Paul-Louis, now a hundred years old and legally blind with his young aide, Dimitri of Yugoslavia, were to join us. I knew that he now owned the Villa Trianon, and Arlene knew that I was dying to see it. When we were about to leave, Arlene told him that I was infatuated with the house and reminisced with him about being there together at one of Elsie's great parties. He had not been in the house for many years but suggested that Dimitri could drive us all out to Versailles to see it. I was thrilled.

When we arrived, Paul-Louis feebly produced an ancient skeleton key from his large key ring and slowly made his way to the gate, attempting unsuccessfully to open it. Within the property was a gatehouse with an apartment for the caretaker on the floor above. Suddenly a wizened old woman dressed in black stuck her head out the window. She hadn't seen her employer in over a decade. She was incredulous: "*Oh, Monsieur le Commandant, Monsieur le Commandant,*" she repeated as she made her way down the stairs to open the creaking gate. She clearly had not been keeping the place up and felt anxious. As Paul-Louis was blind, she needn't have worried.

When I had read the biography, the author described every detail of the interior. The furniture, Elsie's famous striped green and white ceilings, mirrored walls, leopard banquettes. We walked into a house haunted with memories of the past. All of the furniture had been pushed into the corners of the rooms and covered with white sheets. Nothing had been dusted in years. Paul-Louis took Arlene's hand and gazed at the ballroom with his sightless eyes, seeing the room as it must have been decades before.

"Is it just as your remember it?" he asked.

A pregnant pause, and then Arlene responded, "*Exactement.*" It was a moment in time I will never forget.

Manila Shoulders—
Imelda Marcos

Van Cliburn was a lifelong friend of Arlene's whom I had met on several occasions. Van was also a great friend of Philippine dictator Ferdinand Marcos's wife, Imelda. When she was at the height of her power and influence, he had told us many times about her and promised to introduce us. Arlene and I were engaged at the time and living together. I had just gotten home from work, exhausted and looking forward to a quiet night.

As I was changing my clothes, the telephone rang and I heard Arlene say, "Let me ask Marc." She came into the bedroom and told me Van was on the phone. He had just received a call from Imelda Marcos on her private plane, inviting us all to dinner that night at her suite in the Waldorf Towers.

"God, I am so tired, I don't think so," I said.

"Are you crazy? Don't you want to meet her after all of the stories about her jewels, her shoes, and her charisma?"

I thought about it for a split second and said, "You're right, let's go!"

Van and his ever-present mother, Rildia Bee, picked us up in their limo. Imelda's suite in the Waldorf Towers seemed to be the size of the White House, the drawing room lined with five-foot-tall flower arrangements with cards clearly displayed from the Reagans, Henry Kissinger, and so on. Philippine television was filming us.

Ladies-in-waiting fluttered about in national costumes and, finally, there was Imelda, resplendent in a deep blue satin ball gown with her famous Filipino butterfly sleeves set off by a parure of Van Cleef & Arpels diamond and sapphire hidden-setting jewelry. Wow! What a sight. What beauty, what charm. What a show!

We were just twelve for dinner, with a white-gloved footman behind each chair. I sat to Imelda's left and Van to her right—pretty heady for a thirty-two-year old. She was totally in control of the conversation, the First Lady of the Philippines with a personality to match. She discussed world leaders' pros and cons, her cultural plans for her country, et cetera. Then, when the entrée dishes were cleared, she excused herself and came back with small boxes, which she placed on my charger and Arlene's. Oh God, I thought, a souvenir from the Philippines, probably made of capiz shell, which I loathed. *Au contraire!* Arlene's gift was a large pearl and diamond cocktail ring, and there was a pearl and diamond stud set for me. Not shabby!

As we left the dining room to listen to Imelda sing an aria or three, Arlene quietly came up behind me, poked me in the butt with her knee and said, "Still sorry you came?"

Steinway Shoulders—
Van Cliburn

Over fifty years after Arlene first laid eyes on Van Cliburn, he asked her to tell the story of their first meeting on a TV special on his life being filmed for A&E. Arlene had first met Cliburn at the wedding rehearsal dinner given by the parents of her then-fiancé, Lex Barker, at their Park Avenue apartment. Mrs. Barker had called Juilliard for a student to play her piano during dinner. It turned out to be Van Cliburn, an impressionable young man and a big fan of Arlene's.

After dinner she came and sat next to him on the piano bench. He blushed when she told him that "he would become a big star." He went on to be the first American to win the Tchaikovsky Prize in Russia during the height of the Cold War and became an American hero. (The judges had to ask Khrushchev's permission to give an American the prize). He was even given a ticker tape parade in New York City.

After the special was aired, he came back to New York for a visit and took us to dinner at 21 with his partner, Tommy, and Liza Minnelli. The next day he had lunch alone with Arlene. She told him I was taking piano lessons and hunting for a used baby grand piano for our apartment. Van said I should buy a Steinway. It was the only piano he used. Arlene told him I was looking for a second-hand Steinway S, which was their smallest baby grand and would fit nicely in our apartment. It would still cost a bundle. When I returned home from the office, I went directly into my dressing room to change.

"How was your lunch with Van?" I asked.

"Oh, it was lovely. I told him you were taking piano lessons and looking for a used Steinway. Go look in the living room."

As I walked toward it, I gasped, for there stood a brand new black Steinway S, a gift from Van. It was like Matisse giving you a painting. A Steinway from Van Cliburn!

Rubbing Revlon's Shoulders—
Charles Revson

My big break came in 1972 when I landed a job at Revlon, one of the leading cosmetics companies in America in those days. The founder, Charles Revson, was a legend. He had started out in 1932 selling nail polish to beauty salons. Revlon expanded rapidly in 1940 when matching lipsticks were added to the line; department stores clamored for the brand. Competing against established beauty lines such as Elizabeth Arden, Charles of the Ritz, and Helena Rubinstein, Revlon entered the fray.

Charles Revson ruled his empire like a mogul, with a trophy wife, a triplex apartment on Park Avenue, and one of the largest yachts afloat, named after his premium beauty brand, Ultima II. Executives and employees quit or were fired at an alarming rate. It is said that at Revlon, terror was the dominant emotion. Yet Revlon was the best, and it attracted talented people.

I found myself as the newcomer in a large, modern design department that produced packaging for a vast array of products. After the recent success of their fragrance Charlie, I was told that a second fragrance was to be added to the line, aimed at a less sophisticated market. A skin lotion called Moon Drops was one of Revlon's best sellers; women swore by it. In 1973, Charles Revson decided to launch a perfume with the same name. Surprisingly, I was assigned to design the bottle. It was my first perfume bottle. I was twenty-six years old, and I had the unbridled confidence of youth.

It is rather astounding, when I think about it, that my first step into the field that would become my life's work was so casual. I had always liked perfume bottles and admired the classic ones that I saw on my mother's dressing table or in store displays, but I had not specifically studied them as an art form. Now I had to design one. I was on my own.

Each week I created new concepts for the Moon Drops bottle and box. My boss, Al Skolnik, would take them to the "Charles meeting," and I would sweat it out, alone in my office, until he returned, sometimes not until seven o'clock in the evening, and would drop the expensive prototypes in a crumpled heap on my desk. When I asked him what Mr. Revson's comments had been, he would shake his head and say, "Just do new designs." Revson could not articulate what he didn't like, so you would just keep showing him new designs until time ran out or he actually accepted something. Not exactly motivating for an eager, insecure young designer.

Just when I was sure I was going to be fired, he chose one of my umpteenth bottle entries. My design for Moon Drops was a vaselike flacon that fit comfortably in the hand, textured with spiraling lines that continued on the gold metal cap. The spiral implied move-ment, suggesting liquid moonlight. Thank you, God!

Sales at Christmas represented nearly half of Revlon's yearly fragrance revenues. Each year, Revlon produced themed Christmas gift sets to be sold in department stores. They contained various per-fumed products in the line and were lavishly packaged so that men could confidently buy them for their wives or girlfriends and be sure of a thrilled reaction. Now I was assigned the daunting task of creating the Moon Drops Christmas Collection. Ever enthusiastic, I set out to find inspiration.

Antique hunting was one of my passions. I spent weekends combing shops and at auctions. One day, while strolling down East Sixtieth Street, I stopped at the window of a fine antique shop to admire a beautiful Chinese export porcelain plate. I knew instinctively that the pattern would be perfect for the "wrap" on my Moon Drops sets. When I went in, the dealer informed me that pattern was very old, called the "tobacco leaf" pattern. He told me I had very discerning taste for a young man. He also told me the price, which was staggering for the time: $175. I did not hesitate and purchased it. I thought that unique, colorful design would give the presentation the opulent look it needed. I devised a hinged box covered in dark green velvet, embossed with a classic Chinese pattern, and I lined it on the inside with paper printed in my own version of the tobacco leaf pattern. My boss loved it and even reimbursed me the cost of the plate, half of my monthly rent.

Soon after, he announced that I would be going with him to present the collection to Mr. Revson at an important pre-Christmas corporate meeting. Fear gripped my heart. This was the man who verbally destroyed even his top executives; I could only imagine what he might do to me. After a sleepless night, I was informed that I was to go up to the conference room to set up for the five o'clock meeting. We were last on the agenda.

The huge room was designed to intimidate, a setting comparable to "the Donald's" boardroom on *Celebrity Apprentice*. There was a hand-tooled white leather map of the world covering an entire wall, marked by gold stars symbolizing Revlon facilities around the world. I set up the collection on shelves a mile away from Charles's "throne" at the head of the table. The room quickly filled with the company big shots, all dressed in Charles's idea of bespoke fashion: black suits, white shirts, and black ties—very *Six Feet Under*. We waited tensely. After at least thirty minutes, a butler came in to announce that Mr. Revson was napping and would arrive after an undetermined period of time. An hour and a half later, Charles strolled in. The butler brought him a cup of tea. We were not even offered water.

The meeting began. Sinking deeper and deeper into my huge leather chair, I witnessed the massacre. Finally, it was Moon Drops Christmas. Revson rose from his seat, walked slowly to our display and peered over his half glasses without speaking. Did he hate it? I was sure my career had ended before it had even started. He strode back to his seat, sat down, turned to my boss, and asked, "Who did this?" My boss replied, "Marc Rosen," pointing down to what remained of me, shrunk in Siberia. Charles stared at me for what seemed an eternity, then spoke three little words I suppose he had never uttered before: "I like it." I heard it in cadence going around the conference table as the executives repeated to each other, "He liked it, he liked it, he liked it." Tough shoulders!

Ten Fendi Shoulders

In 1989, my world changed when Elizabeth Arden acquired the Fendi license for perfume. My boss, the president of Arden, handed them to me on a silver platter, as he was uncomfortable dealing with five demanding Fendi sisters who spoke no English. Yet after about an hour we all had bonded: Anna, Alda, Paola, Franca, and, most of all, Carla, with whom I worked the most to launch their new fragrance.

They were divine, impossible, warm, embracing, obsessive, controlling, and frustrating to the extreme, but I had one of my happiest working experiences and life learning lessons with these crazy, brilliant gals. Branding, a word unheard of then, was already in their blood. They ate, slept, and breathed Fendi. For a year, I received a phone call every morning at nine o'clock from Ann Marie, Carla's right-hand English-speaking assistant. Most days I was ready to kill them, but in the end, I grew as a professional and as a person from this incredible experience. They taught me discipline, focus, and pushing till you hit the wall to achieve your goals. While Carla could drive a person mad, I grew to love and admire her.

Collaboration was their middle name. Before e-mail, they each used a pad with a different color of paper. They would write their thoughts and send them on to the appropriate sister responsible for each area—Carla for marketing, Alda for retail, Anna for design. Paola, the eldest, was president.

In those days, Bloomingdale's was the store to launch a fragrance in New York. They had given Fendi fashion its own corner window on Lexington Avenue. One day, Carla called up to announce that I should go to the president, Marvin Traub, and talk him into using a Fendi shopping bag, printed with the beautiful Fendi fragrance ad created by my colleague Paulette Dufault and the brilliant photographer Sheila Metzner.

This was going to be a tough one. Bloomingdale's was famous for its classic "big brown bag." I went in with some trepidation, but I channeled Carla, who took no prisoners and got him to agree. An even bigger victory was talking him into letting us install specially loomed carpeting with the double "F" logos down the whole center aisle on the cosmetics floor. What a coup!

When the sisters came to New York for the launch, I went out to dinner with them, and after dinner, although it was quite late, we decided to stop by Bloomingdale's to check out the carpets. I expected them to be thrilled, but alas, the stars were crossed. They peered through the windows with smiles and turned back to me with frowns. The color palette was off! They insisted that Arden pay to reweave the carpet. In three days! Otherwise, they said, they would refuse to attend the launch. That is how fanatical they were about every detail of their brand. They were adamant and obsessive, but I learned a big lesson. The devil is in the details.

Dragging Shoulders—
Rhonda Fleming

The "other redhead" in Hollywood making films in the fifties, Rhonda Fleming, was a friend of Arlene's who even shared the same birthdate. They had lost touch over the years, living on different coasts. Arlene called her when she knew we were going to Los Angeles, and she invited us for drinks one evening to meet her new husband, Ted Mann, who at the time was the wealthy owner of a large chain of movie theaters including the historic Grauman's Chinese Theatre movie palace in Hollywood, renamed Mann's Chinese Theatre.

Earlier that day, we were shopping at Neiman Marcus in Beverly Hills. I was picking up a new suit in the men's department just adjacent to women's shoes, where Arlene was browsing. When I had the suit, I walked toward the down escalator where Arlene was waiting, and witnessed the following scene. A frowsy-looking woman was coming down the escalator wearing a curly red wig, heavy makeup, and a too-tight knit dress topped with tons of junk jewelry. She saw Arlene and went mad.

"Oh my God, it's Rhonda Fleming. You are my favorite movie star. Everyone says I look just like you."

Arlene calmly smiled and replied that she was not Rhonda. The woman still riding the escalator took another look and exclaimed, "I can't believe it, you're Arlene Dahl. I am so sorry. I love you too. I'll let you in on a little secret: I'm a man. How'm I doing, honey?"

Arlene, not missing a beat or showing any surprise, gave her or him the OK hand sign and said, "Keep up the good work." The person moved on, and we fell apart.

We couldn't wait to meet Rhonda and Ted to tell them the serendipitous story. Can you imagine this occurring on the very day we were to see the real Rhonda? We arrived and after a few pleasantries recounted the story. Rhonda roared and Ted went silent. This man had no sense of humor and was probably homophobic. Arlene couldn't imagine living with someone so dour. He died a year later, leaving Rhonda millions. I guess that made up for his lack of humor. Rhonda had the last laugh.

Shoulder to Shoulder—
Bruce Weber

Bruce Weber started his fashion career as a model. I first met him in 1971 while I was working as a young package designer at my first job, a boutique studio in New York. They had just landed the Julius Schmid account. The company was noted as the country's foremost manufacturer of condoms. With names like "Sheik" and "Ramses," they were slightly dated, to say the least. To compound their marketing problem, in the early seventies, before venereal diseases became prevalent and AIDS became an epidemic, women were on the pill and men were not using condoms.

A new package design was deemed the answer. I envisioned foil packets and cartons featuring "tasteful" romantic scenes of attractive young couples embracing by the fireside or in the park. The budget for photography was slim. After viewing several portfolios, I called Nan Bush, an agent representing several photographers. She suggested a new client of hers, a former male model, Bruce, who wanted to become a photographer and would work for a small fee, as he was anxious to build a portfolio. Well, Bruce became one of the most famous photographers ever.

I don't know if our designs made sales soar, but the project became serendipitous for all of us. Bruce and Nan have been life partners all these years. We have remained good friends, bonded by this unlikely start to our careers. I guess we have done pretty well for ourselves considering this inauspicious beginning.

LEATHER SHOULDERS

I was twenty-four, just married. New New York City apartment across from the Morgan Library, just back from our honeymoon in Italy, first day on a new job in the cosmetics industry. I took the Madison Avenue bus feeling a bit nervous about making good on the job. I was seated across from a bench. We stopped to pick up passengers. A woman came on and sat directly across from me. "*Why me, God?*" She was dressed in dominatrix drag: black leather, black slicked-back hair, harlequin white makeup with round red circles painted on her cheeks, and turquoise eye shadow up to her eyebrows, which along with her upper and lower lashes were blackened with heavy mascara and eyeliner. And to complete the ensemble, she was wielding a huge bullwhip! This was one angry broad. I kept repeating to myself, "Stay calm, do not stare at her." But my eyes would not listen. A morbid fascination brought them back to her each time I tried to look at the scenery. Finally, my worst fear was realized, and she burst out in anger, screaming, "Stop staring at me, you bastard."

I knew all was lost until I heard the guy next to me cursing at her. She was attacking my seatmate, not me. The bus driver stopped and escorted her off. Rubbing shoulders can be dangerous.

GEISHA SHOULDERS

The Japanese are amazing hosts, but to the point of obsession. On a business trip to Japan years ago while I was at Elizabeth Arden, I was in Nagoya working with a porcelain company that would be manufacturing a collection I had designed based upon the Topkapi Palace in Istanbul.

I was there with a few colleagues and very stressed and tired. We spent each day struggling with the language problem, the price issues with each piece, the supplier trying to "dumb down" the designs, and my protecting their integrity. Each night, when I dreamed of having dinner alone or with my staff in the hotel, they politely persisted in taking us out to dinner.

On the last day, when I was completely spent, I decided to take a stand by refusing to join them no matter how hard they persisted. They looked crestfallen, and my group made me feel I would be insulting them if I didn't go. I begrudgingly agreed, knowing I would be sorry.

After an endless dinner—Nagoya was hardly the culinary capital of Japan—I prayed that we could go back to the hotel and crash. We were walking down a congested street that looked like New York's Forty-Second Street before the cleanup, when suddenly a sleazy-looking man appeared out of nowhere and gestured toward a small alley. I was sure our hosts would ignore him. Wrong! The next thing I knew we were being hustled down the narrow path to a building with a low doorway. I was hostile to the extreme, feeling coerced and controlled against my will. On the other hand, my colleagues were all for it. I had a moment and realized I would be ruining everyone's fun if I pulled rank. I decided to get with the program and walked in. We were greeted by a guy who announced in heavily accented English that we were in a "touché feelé" bar. It was hard to keep a straight face. The space was very compact with low ceilings, divided between a large banquette and two small booths.

Suddenly, out of nowhere, six girls appeared wearing pastel negligees. The host, sensing I was the boss, introduced me to a petite, very pretty gal and ushered us into a booth. Meanwhile the guys were all seated with the other five girls on the banquette having a ball. Sake was plentiful.

My favorite geisha and I were getting to know each other, but as she spoke no English and giggled at the end of each phrase and I spoke no Japanese, we both focused on our sake. Being a proper Japanese courtesan, she poured the sake into square wooden cups. We toasted and sipped, but with no way of communicating, we began drinking in earnest.

After our third sake I realized that there was piped music playing. Feeling no pain, I agreed to dance to a couple tunes, but just as I thought we should sit down, my little cutie pointed up to the ceiling with enthusiasm. Of course, I thought, this place is so small that it must be the precursor to a larger space upstairs with bedrooms, and she is certainly indicating that I join her. In a moment of clarity I realized I was a guest of our supplier and needed to let him know I was going upstairs to sample my gal's charms. After all, this was described as a "touché feelé" bar. When I indicated my plan with a wink to my host, he looked at me quizzically and asked me to describe her invitation. I explained how she had pointed to the ceiling, while my staff was listening with great interest.

He asked her in Japanese her intentions. She shook her head and stammered her explanation. My host turned to me and said, "I am sorry, but when she held up her finger she simply meant, 'one more dance.'"

Everyone burst into laughter. I was embarrassed but amused. My hot night in Nagoya turned out to be cold sushi.

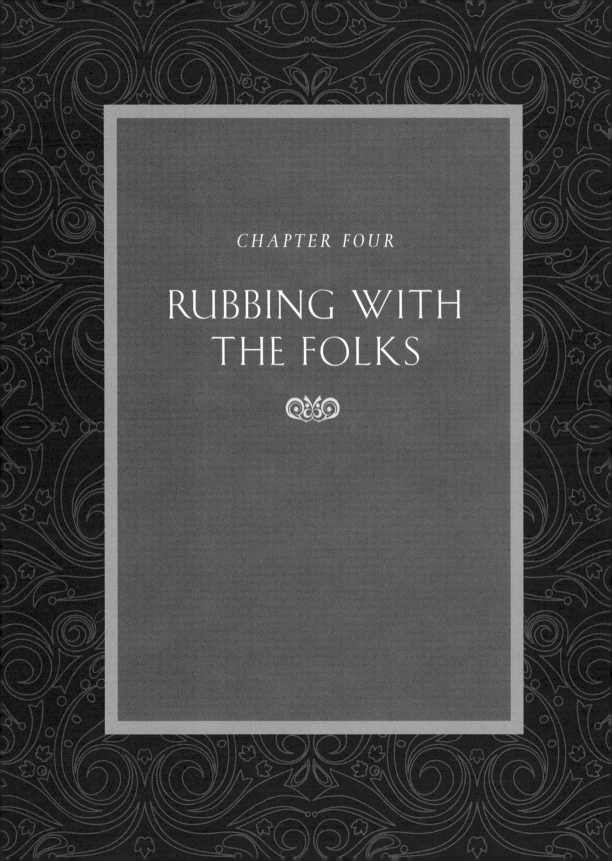

CHAPTER FOUR

RUBBING WITH THE FOLKS

Mona Lisa's Shoulders— With Susan Lloyd in Palm Beach

Arlene and I have had homes in Palm Beach, Florida, for over three decades. It is a very special place where big money, old-fashioned good manners, aesthetics, and eccentricity rule—my kind of place. Last year I found myself down there for a few days on business. I had accepted an invitation to attend a cocktail party at the handsome Ralph Lauren store for a book signing of Hilary Geary Ross and Harry Benson's new coffee-table book, *Palm Beach People*.

I had a business dinner with two colleagues afterwards. Before leaving, I ran into Susan Lloyd, a good friend whose family owns the Marlborough Gallery. She asked me if I wanted to join her and a few friends for dinner alfresco in the charming courtyard at Via Mizner. I told her I would have loved to but already had an engagement. When I got into my car, my cell phone rang. It was one of the people I was to meet for dinner. She had to cancel. I drove over to the Palm Beach Grill, a very popular spot where you have to promise your firstborn to get a reservation. The noise level was deafening, and as I was waiting for my guest, I was pushed and shoved in the very active bar scene. My guest was fifteen minutes late, so I called. He told me he was also unable to join me. I was not amused. I was hungry and doubly stood up. Poor me!

I left and decided to drive over to see if Susan still wanted me for dinner. She was very gracious and had a chair brought over so I could join her group. It was a beautiful evening, made

SUSAN LLOYD, MONA LISA (THE PIG)

even nicer by the fact that it was snowing back home in New York. Via Mizner is the crown jewel of Worth Avenue, built by architect Addison Mizner, the creative genius who designed most the palatial Palm Beach mansions from 1915 to 1930. He built Via Mizner to simulate a Mediterranean village of shops, along with his home, a triplex within a tower, with each entrance flanked by two enormous glass and wrought-iron doors. Our table was situated right next to the doors.

Shortly after I sat down, the door opened and a man came out to offer us a good bottle of his wine. He was Nicholas Thomas, a friend of Susan's and the owner of the house. He went back inside, leaving the large door ajar. Susan asked if I had met Mona Lisa.

"No," I answered. "Who is she?"

"A pig. They have a pet pig!"

"You're making this up," I said.

"I am not—that guy has a black and white pig living with them who is divine."

With that, I glanced over to the foyer and saw a pig walk gingerly down the beautiful staircase, put her snout through the opening of the door, and push it open. Mona Lisa sauntered down to our table and presented herself to say hello. She had better manners than a lot of people I know. I petted her and said hello. I, such a city boy, had never before seen an actual pig in person. Susan made a huge fuss, singing a few bars of Nat King Cole's famous song. They brought over a doggie-type bed for Mona to lie in and a plate of broccoli that Aunt Susan hand-fed to Mona. My Palm Beach evening had really turned into a "pig-out."

SOUTHERN SHOULDERS

For my next Christmas porcelain collection for Arden, I decided to work with an American museum or great manor house. After the Pavilion at Brighton, Versailles, and the Topkapi Palace, it would be quite a challenge. I called Wendell Garrett, publisher of *The Magazine Antiques*, for advice. He suggested that I select the magnificent plantation homes of Natchez, Mississippi. He went on to explain that although the inhabitants were loath to admit it, Natchez was saved from destruction during the Civil War because they were Yankee sympathizers. Wendell told me that the homes, all privately owned, were on tour under the auspices of the Pilgrimage Garden Club. He gave me the name of the lady who was the head of the club. I called to see if they would host our visit and allow me to bring my assistant and a photographer to be inspired to create the collection. When she heard the name "Elizabeth Arden," she was putty in my hands.

"Of course," she drawled. "Y'all are welcome any old taime!"

I was so excited. Ever since I first saw *Gone with the Wind* I had been a devotee of the Old South. Magnolias, Spanish moss, and Ionic columns were all right up my alley. Lannie Hart, my assistant, was from Virginia. I couldn't understand why she wasn't as enthusiastic as I was.

Soon, I knew why. The club president I had spoken to was to meet us at the airport with her husband. After changing planes in Atlantic, we then had to take a puddle jumper.

We picked up our bags and waited outside the door to the small local airport, exhausted but prepared for the three-hour drive to Natchez. Suddenly, a large turquoise Cadillac with fins pulled up. Our host, a nice middle-aged southern matron welcomed us with great southern charm and introduced us to her husband, Beauregard, who sported a handlebar mustache, a caricature of a carpetbagger during Reconstruction. They suggested that we stop for dinner along the way. They wound up drinking theirs. A few cocktails, bourbon (of course), wine, and several after-dinner drinks.

Just as I was trying not to make eye contact with Lannie and wondering how Beauregard would ever be able to drive—in the dark, no less—I soon found out. We got back into the Caddy and pulled back onto the road. I looked out the car window and saw headlights coming toward us. Oh my God, we were in the wrong lane. Beau swerved back into the right lane just in time. Now we were in for the *long* ride to Natchez. To make conversation, I thought I would tell them that Arlene, a good friend of the actor George Hamilton, had arranged for me to have drinks with his brother Bill, a noted interior decorator who had purchased and saved an antebellum home in Natchez. Wrong! Turns out they would rather have the dilapidated house crumble over a fourth-generation Natchez family than be saved and renovated in the best of taste by a newcomer, especially a gay decorator. To make matters worse, all the way to Natchez, they told us about their bigotry toward blacks and Jews. Did they know that Rosen was a Jewish name? I was sure I would wind up being tarred and feathered and run out of town on a rail!

We finally arrived at Stanton Hall, the headquarters of the venerable Pilgrimage Garden Club. It was midnight, and our first house tour would take place at 10:00 a.m. Breakfast at 9:00. Stanton Hall was part of the house tour package that tourists looking for a bit of the Old South could sign up for.

We entered the enormous, dark mansion and walked up the grand carved wooden staircase to a huge center foyer off of which were the bedrooms. I was shown to the Lincoln bedroom, complete with a large four-poster bed. Lannie had the room next door. Her bedroom had a bathroom, en suite; mine did not. I had to walk into the center hall to access one. I opened my luggage, left it on the floor, and fell into a coma.

The next morning, I woke up with a start, realizing I was late. I bolted out of the room into the hall bathroom. I quickly showered, shaved, and opened the door prepared to enter my bedroom and get dressed. Quite to my surprise, I found out that the house tour had already begun and there were fifty tourists greeting me in my bathrobe. Not an auspicious beginning.

Well, having shrugged off my initial encounter, we met our Garden Club guide and proceeded on our tour of the old plantations. I felt as if I were a prisoner in a Stephen Foster songbook. It was now nine o'clock and we were arriving at a lovely home with a columned portico.

We were met by the family, who were very pleased to receive us. After being told the history of the house and given the tour, we were asked if we would like a Bloody Mary. It was only 10:30 a.m., so I politely declined. We thanked them and rode on to the next house, equally beautiful and historic. Another pleasant group of family members who again kindly offered us Bloody Marys. It must have been the Natchez signature drink. On the way to the next manse, our charming guide politely explained Mississippi protocol.

"Mr. Rooosen," she drawled, "when you all are offered a Bloody Mary at the next house, please accept because, you see, sir, they all want a Bloody Mary but won't have one themselves if their guests refuse. Southern manner, you see."

God, I thought, if they start with drinks at ten o'clock, how were they faring by dinnertime? Turned out their alcoholism rate was through the roof.

By the third day, the charm of the Old South had definitely worn off. I took half a Valium to get through the morning. That evening we were invited to the annual Pilgrimage Festival. All of the food was fried, including the pickles. Where was Nathan's? Then it happened: the entertainment, the last straw, "Tableaus of the Civil War," except in the Natchez version (remember the guilt) the South had won. Damn you, Robert E. Lee, enough was enough. We high-tailed it back to Yankee land in a hurry. The South shall rise again. Save those Dixie cups.

A Cabbie's Shoulders

While this may not fit into the category of rubbing shoulders with celebrities, it does fit into my theme of how being open to everything and everyone can bring you fascinating slices of life.

For me, riding in a New York City taxicab is all about transportation, not about conversation. I say good morning or good day when I get in and then offer the location. When I first started riding taxis, the drivers were generally Jewish. Over the years the nationalities have gone from Japanese to Arab to Russian. Usually I look at the ID cards located on the partition when I get in just in case I've been kidnapped.

One day after entering a cab, the cheery driver said, "Today is my last day of driving a taxi. I have been doing it for sixty years, and the wife and I have decided to pack it in, sell our house in Queens, and move south."

I glanced first at him and then at the ID card and realized that he was an older Jewish gentleman named Harold Goldberg. So, picking up on his enthusiasm and thinking of my father, I said, "How nice, are you moving to Boca?"

"Oh, no," he said. "We will be living on our new boat in the Caymans."

A nice older Jewish couple living on a boat on an island known as a tax haven? Having just finished John Grisham's *The Client*, which took place on Grand Cayman, I replied, "Did you know that island was a place where wealthy people park their assets as a tax shelter?"

"Oh yes," the driver said. "Our lawyer and accountant suggested that we move there." He continued, "Do you know how much a taxi medallion is worth?"

"$250,000," I guessed.

"$450,000," he said. Okay, so he sold his little house in Queens, and his medallion, very nice but…the Grand Caymans?

Harold continued, "During the Depression, I bought fifty of them, just sold them last week."

As my mind was now ringing up sales like a cash register, he went on, "Do you know the block on Tenth Avenue between Eighteenth and Nineteenth Streets?"

"Yes," I replied.

"Well, that was mine. Do you know the row of brownstones between Sixth and Seventh Avenues on Twenty-Second Street? Sold them too."

My total was now into the multimillions when he pulled up to my stop. I paid the fare and said, "Good luck, Harold, and I don't think you need my tip!"

Weight Watchers Shoulders— Jean Nidetch

Years ago, I met Jean Nidetch, the founder of Weight Watchers, and we liked each other. She was a big, brash, blond lady with moxie to spare and an ego the size of Pittsburgh, but fun and likable and lonely.

A few years before, she had sold the company to Heinz for a fortune and was their international spokesperson. At dinner in a Manhattan restaurant I was curious to see what she was ordering. I expected carrot sticks, salad, no dressing, and broiled fish. In fact, she ordered a normal meal that was a good mix of carbohydrates and protein but was definitely not a "diet meal." Throwing caution to the wind, I ordered a Caesar salad, pasta Bolognese, and a chocolate soufflé for dessert: very un–Weight Watchers.

As each course was served, I noticed that she was helping herself to my plate. When she had helped herself to half of my soufflé, I finally said, "Jean, if you want dessert, why didn't your order one?"

"Don't be silly," she said. "Don't you know that there are no calories if you eat off someone else's plate?"

SHRUNKEN SHOULDERS

When I was twenty-nine and going through a divorce, I thought I should see a shrink to talk about my conflicted feelings. Even though I asked for the divorce, I cared for my wife and felt guilty about the split.

I was referred to a psychiatrist on Central Park West. Her office was in a brownstone where she also lived. When I arrived for my first appointment I was buzzed in and found myself in a dark, dingy waiting room with low ceilings on the ground level of the house. It was furnished in very bad Danish modern furniture from the sixties, one of my all-time least favorite periods of furniture design. Brown was the dominant color, with carpeting way beyond "shabby chic" condition.

After waiting for half an hour, the doctor sent a signal for me to come upstairs to her office, which was clearly done by the same nondecorator.

My experience with all doctors, other than plastic surgeons, is that they are both nonaesthetic and cheap, a terrible combination. She was very nice and professional and I continued seeing her for a few months.

One day, knowing I was a designer, after our time was up she asked me if I knew where to have furniture re-upholstered. I seized the moment and asked her if she had deliberately done the waiting room in "dour decor" so that if patients were not sufficiently depressed when they entered, sitting down there would do the trick.

She looked at me in amazement, not knowing what I meant. I continued, knowing this would probably be my last visit. I decided to go for it.

"Well, you must realize that between the low ceilings, dirty brown carpeting, and worn furnishings, it is not an uplifting experience sitting there."

Giving it some thought, she said, "Well, can you help me redecorate it?"

"Yes," I answered, "but my fee is commensurate with your hourly fee times fifty."

She said she would think about it. I guess she's still thinking.

COMMON SHOULDERS

After joining Elizabeth Arden in 1977, I enjoyed getting to know my colleagues. One of the marketing directors was a gal named Sue Sargenson. She was in charge of skin care. One day she was meeting with me in my office and we got to talking about our private lives. I was just going through a divorce, and I asked her if she had ever been married. She said she had years before and that Sargenson was her married name. Curious, I asked her what her maiden name was.

"Oh, it was common," she said.

"Was it Smith or Brown?" I offered.

"No, it was common."

"I'll bet it was Green or Jones," I answered.

"Marc, my name was Sue Common! Why do you think I got married?"

CHAPTER FIVE

RUBBING WITH
THE STARS

(DIVAS)

Wet Shoulders—Esther Williams

Esther Williams, MGM's famous Million Dollar Mermaid, was quite infamous in our family.

Fanny Brice once said, "Wet, she's a star. Dry, she's not." But in our book she was "all wet," period!

When Arlene joined the studio, they became good friends. When she married *Tarzan* star Lex Barker, they double dated with Esther and her then-husband, Ben Gage. Esther became "infatuated" with Fernando Lamas, recently signed to a contract. The Argentine heartthrob made his screen test with Arlene, and they became quite an item. This did not sit well with Esther. Eventually they got married and had a son, Lorenzo Lamas, and Esther was, shall we say, "not amused." She used her considerable clout to costar with him in her next picture, *Dangerous When Wet*, appropriately named! The rest is history, and soon after, Arlene filed for divorce.

As the studio veered toward making the new breed of "kitchen sink" movies and the public tired of Esther's films, MGM did not renew her lucrative contract. With "Latin lover" films also out of fashion, Fernando found himself at liberty as well. Leaving her husband and three little children, Esther moved to Rome with Fernando and worked on Spaghetti Westerns. In the end they returned, and after eight years of marriage she started a new career endorsing swimming pools, bathing suits, and gained fifty pounds. Fernando became a good director.

For some reason, in spite of her fame and the acquisition of the

Lamas name, Esther obsessively loathed Arlene. She systematically poisoned Lorenzo's mind against his own mother, while her own children refused to speak to her. All the stuff of B-movies, the rift continued for decades. After Lorenzo's first and second marriages, when both wives met Arlene and Esther, they set him straight as to which was the "keeper."

While Arlene and I were engaged and Lorenzo was starring on TV in *Falcon Crest*, Fernando was diagnosed with pancreatic cancer and died within a few weeks. Lorenzo was destroyed, as he worshipped his dad. He called the day after the funeral to ask Arlene to call Esther with condolences. They had not spoken for decades. Stories of Esther still trashing Arlene in Los Angeles were continually coming to light, but Arlene, ever the lady, dialed the number. She asked if I would like to pick up the extension and listen in. Would I!

Esther started out pleasantly playing the bereaved widow. After a minute or two she began putting down Victoria, the lovely gal Lorenzo was married to.

"All she cares about is shopping," said Esther, having just buried her beloved. "She reminds me of you!"

But the best story took place years later at a party in Manhattan given by impresario David Gest, destined to be the future husband of Liza Minnelli. We had known David for years in Los Angeles as the very successful producer of major "movie star" fundraiser galas for the Motion Picture Home. Each year David invited every star, even the ones you thought were dead, to an all-expenses-paid weekend each year to attend this wonderful event.

He had moved to Manhattan and organized a big party at his new condo. Esther was among the other guests. Over the years when we attended these or similar "Old Hollywood" dos, Esther and Arlene miraculously never made eye contact. Conversely, whenever she saw me, she would kill me with kindness and tell me how wonderful Lorenzo had said I was. She was what I would call terminally insincere, like a disease. This evening at David's was no exception. Seated around a low cocktail table, Esther decided to sit in the chair next to mine to visit. I looked around the room to see where my wife was, desperate to be saved. She was across the room, deep in conversation.

I had just read that Esther was writing her autobiography and thought it would be a fine topic to bring up, as it was all about her! She held my hand with deep feeling (perhaps she really could act when dry) and proceeded to give me the nitty-gritty on the progress of her book. She was working with cowriter Digby Diehl, with whom she was clearly not happy. Her face contorted as she told me that she had read his first draft and hated it.

"I told him he was a pussy."

Was I hearing things, or was Esther Williams, the star of MGM's highest-grossing movies, admired by millions of fans, actually using that word? I didn't blush.

"I told him that I would give him a story that would really sell this book, give it some teeth."

She went on, whipping herself into a frenzy reviling this poor, castrated soul.

In the end, Esther threw handsome, virile actor Jeff Chandler under the bus, writing that while they were having an affair she discovered he was a cross-dresser. If Jeff weren't already dead, this would have killed him, but his children and grandchildren were alive and very hurt. The story was not true, according to many of his closest friends, who cut Esther off—among them Merv Griffin, who was to have hosted her book party at his hotel, the Beverly Hilton. As I said, terminally insincere.

SHIRLEY EDER, GINGER ROGERS

HOLLYWOOD SHOULDERS

The great producer Alexander Cohen, who had previously done *Night of 100 Stars*, was at it again, producing a television special, *Happy Birthday, Hollywood*, to celebrate its hundredth birthday. It was to be televised live from the Shrine Auditorium in Los Angeles. In his inimitable style, Alex pulled out all the stops and invited Arlene and every star of her generation to appear. *Dynasty* fashion designer Nolan Miller was dressing each one in a variation of evening dresses, all in ecru silk and lace for a Victorian gazebo sequence. But the real action was happening backstage. These great stars, who were used to having gorgeous dressing rooms at their studios, were sharing and enjoying it.

During the intermission I went back to visit Arlene, who was dressing with Alice Faye, Cyd Charisse, and Lana Turner. Alice quipped that they should be members of a club, as they had all been married to the same men at one time or another: Alice and Cyd to Tony Martin, Arlene and Lana to Lex Barker, and so on. Lucille Ball came in to tell Arlene that she had just told Esther Williams off. Ann Miller was sharing with Jane Powell and Kathryn Grayson, and she was hogging the dressing table.

I decided to say hello to Ginger Rogers, who was also featured in the first-act scene wearing a lovely ecru gown. Ginger, bless her heart, had the world's worst taste. Too froufrou, with "Baby Jane" yellow hair. I couldn't find her anywhere. Finally one of the dressers told me she was hiding in the very back of the stage behind several rows of curtain drops. Now curious, I made my way back to find her. She smiled and put her finger up to her mouth to say *shhh!* She wanted to wear her own dress for the finale and knew that Alex would not approve of her straying from the approved look. She looked like Little Bo Peep, wearing an enormous hoopskirt ball gown in bright taxicab yellow and green. All she needed was a staff. She had a green ribbon with a large yellow silk poppy tied around her neck and ribbons in her hair—a sight to be sure! Nolan Miller would commit suicide. I told her she looked wonderful and made a hasty retreat. "Girls, Glorious Girls!"

A Soprano's Shoulders—
Anna Moffo

On our twelfth wedding anniversary, our friends John and Suzanne Mados generously offered to host a big party at their hotel in New York called the Wyndham. I was asked to orchestrate the entertainment. I threw myself into the effort by asking several close friends to each grace us with a song. Everyone I asked said yes immediately. Our dear friend Liliane Montevecchi, who had just won the Tony Award for her amazing rendition of "Folies Bergère" in the Broadway musical *Nine*, said, "*Absolument!*" Metropolitan Opera star Patrice Munsel said, "Of course, dahling." Our friend Jenny Gucci of the Gucci Guccis said, "*Non c'è problema,*" and so on.

I phoned our friend Anna Moffo, who was known as America's most beautiful mezzo-soprano, and she said that unfortunately she was going to be doing a concert in Philadelphia. Of course I understood.

Everything was going smoothly, with eighty-plus guests having accepted. About two weeks before the party, Anna called to say the gig in Philly had been postponed and she would be pleased to come to sing at the party if she could perform first. No one else had made any demands, but I said, "Of course, Anna." She said she wanted to sing "It's a Grand Night for Singing," and I told her it was my favorite song. I began feeling a twinge of concern but ignored it.

Two days before the party, she called to ask if we had someone to accompany her, with whom she could rehearse beforehand. I wanted to say *no*, knowing the way this was going. I called Jenny Gucci to beg her to lend her fellow to la Moffo. She graciously agreed, and I put them together, thinking all was well.

The big night arrived, and as Arlene and I made our way through the hotel doors, Alan the accompanist greeted us to say that he had never experienced anyone like Anna before—every inch a total diva! I thanked him and told him how much we appreciated his efforts.

"I doubt if she'll sing," he said. At this point, I really didn't care.

The room looked beautiful, our host and hostess made lovely toasts, and we had champagne and caviar to start. Now the program was to begin. Anna was announced with fanfare. She looked beautiful, but when her song began, she was completely off-key! Anna Moffo off-key? Impossible. Since I am practically tone-deaf, I assumed it was me. Not so: everyone was looking at the flowers, trying not to react to the flat and sharp tones. Anna never knew. "A Grand Night for Singing" turned out to be not so grand.

RUBBING ZORBA'S SHOULDERS—
ANTHONY QUINN

Tony Quinn, a great friend of ours, was married to an impossible Italian woman named Jolanda. She had been a dresser in the wardrobe department during the filming of his epic biblical film *Barabbas*. Over the years she elevated her position to costume designer. She also billed herself as a countess. Their affair produced three sons. Tony had been married to Katherine DeMille, the daughter of famed movie director Cecil B. DeMille, and they had two or three children. In fact, he had so many affairs over the years we lost count of how many offspring he had produced.

He was a wonderful and fascinating man, sensitive yet gruff, funny yet solemn. His personal history made up several autobiographies. He was prolific in many ways—the number of films, plays, books, paintings, sculptures, and awards he had won. Half-Irish, half-Mexican, he had emigrated from Tijuana with his mother to Los Angeles absolutely penniless. His story is remarkable. He had a cleft palette and entered a competition for an architecture prize in high school. Frank Lloyd Wright was the judge. Noticing Tony's infirmity, he paid for a surgery to correct the problem and afterwards suggested that he take acting lessons to get his speech back correctly. To earn money, he became an extra on the Paramount lot and was cast as an Indian by DeMille. The rest is history.

I never tired of his Hollywood stories. At our many dinners

ANTHONY QUINN

at Le Cirque he would regale us with incidents from his career, Jolanda would invariably interrupt to correct him, and an argument would ensue. Ever jealous, whenever he mentioned a female costar or acquaintance, she would remark in a thick Italian accent, "She whore." It could have been anyone from Jacqueline Kennedy Onassis to Sophia Loren. A woman with a huge ego, she nonetheless seemed to like Arlene, certain that she had never slept with Tony.

A favorite story of mine took place during my experience working with the five Fendi sisters, launching their signature fragrance. I had decided to launch it at a big party at the beautiful Burden Mansion in New York with a gala called Carnivale Fendi, as the date following the end of Lent was a huge deal in Rome, where the five Fendi sisters were from. Since I wanted celebrities there and frankly needed a famous actor to be photographed with these girls, I asked the Quinns. Jolanda was thrilled because she had lived in Rome and claimed that Carla Fendi was a close friend. Tony was less thrilled, especially when he found out that it was black tie.

Jolanda called me to cry that Tony didn't want to come but I should ask him because she thought he would do it for me. As I was juggling the five sisters and the insane details of the Bloomingdale's launch, plus parties all over the country, I was not in the mood, but I dialed the number, prepared to use up a whole week's worth of charm.

"Tony, I have you seated between Arlene and Gina Lollobrigida," knowing he would love this.

I realized he was only torturing Jolanda, as she was desperate to come. It worked. The night of the event, glam to the extreme, we took the said pictures during cocktails. I seated Jolanda to my left, which was a real sacrifice.

On the way in to dinner, Jolanda, who had already scoped out the tables, rushed up to me and said, "You have to change the seating, Tony only wants to sit next to me." Right!

I guess he must have slept with Gina at some point. I ignored her, and a good time was had by all. The next morning, she called to say thank you. Jolanda, who had olive skin and was attractive but not a great beauty, said "Arleeene looked sooo beautiful. She has the most beauuutiful skin in the world—next to mine."

Don't you love it!

Secret Shoulders—
More Quinn

We would have dinner with the Quinns on a regular basis, joined by other friends. I would usually call Tony's secretary, Kathy, to schedule. She sounded youngish, lovely, and bright. It was a great way to make plans without having to deal with Jolanda, who was exhausting. One day, while she was in Rome visiting her married son, Tony called to invite us for dinner. Little did we know he had a secret to share.

After some dinner chatter, he explained that, since we were close friends, he wanted to share some news before it came out in the press. He had been having an affair for some time with Kathy, and she was pregnant. He was planning to tell Jolanda upon her return that week. Wow, what a bombshell! We told him how much we appreciated his confidence and that we would support him no matter what.

A few weeks later, Arlene hosted a birthday dinner for me with about eighteen people. We were seated at a long table in a private room at a lovely restaurant called the Box Tree. The Quinns came in spite of the news. It was getting major press, with Jolanda being very vocal about her feelings. There was certainly an elephant in the room. I was seated at one end of the table, with Jane Powell on one side and Carol Channing, who is hard of hearing and speaks very loudly, on the other. Tony was at the other end next to Arlene and a few seats apart from Jolanda, who was seated next to Charles Lowe, Carol's husband. Carol, who had read about the Quinn drama, asked me which lady was Mrs. Quinn.

"She is seated at Charles's right," I answered.

She got up and walked over to him and said in a stage whisper, "Please don't say anything to Mrs. Quinn about the baby!"

Stunned silence, and then Tony broke up and so did we all. Jolanda was not amused.

DANCING SHOULDERS— ANN MILLER

In the early eighties, one of Broadway's biggest hit musicals was *Sugar Babies*, starring MGM's Mickey Rooney and Ann Miller. A burlesque takeoff, it was a huge success. Ann, an old friend of Arlene's from the studio days, came back into our lives now that she was working in New York. After doing the show for over a year, she called to say she was going to be made a dame by the Knights of Malta and we were invited to her investiture at Christ Church on Park Avenue at 11:00 p.m. after the show. We accepted with pleasure but were skeptical about their provenance. Who the hell were the Knights of Malta?

Ann was a terrific personality who tap-danced and sang up a storm but was rather spacey. I called our friend Eugenia Sheppard, then the town's most powerful social columnist. She knew everything. Eugenia called back after doing a little research and told me there were two orders of the Knights of Malta: one very prestigious and the other a renegade group that was completely déclassé. Ann unfortunately did not know the difference. She was so impressed with being made a dame that she had failed to ask "Dame of what?"

On the appointed night, we arrived at the church half an hour before Ann's entrance. As we slid into a pew we noticed that we were sharing it with the likes of Ethel Merman, Anne Francine, Celeste Holm, and Earl Blackwell. The church's altar was set up like a stage, with a gilded throne in the center. Sitting on the altar and on either side was a strange group of characters dressed in medieval drag. Now it became apparent to us all that we were in for quite a time. When the woman singing strange gothic hymns had finished, a man dressed as a page thumped his staff on the stone floor and announced Miss Ann Miller. We all turned around to cheer her on, but alas it was not our girl, who stood five foot ten in heels, but dear Helen Hayes, who was barely five feet. Poor Helen was searching for a seat and never knew the irony. Well, we all lost it. In a stage whisper, Ethel began singing "There Is Nothing Like a Dame" from *South Pacific*.

After a few minutes the page was told that Ann was, in fact, waiting to make her entrance, and he made the announcement again with great aplomb. Ann, who thought this ceremony akin to being presented in the Court of St. James, had ordered a scarlet velvet cape with a train edged in ermine tails for the occasion. She made her way down the aisle as if in a scene from *Elizabeth the Queen*, knelt down, and was knighted. What a night!

Sassy Shoulders—
Joan Collins, David Gest

Joan Collins is one of my favorite people. She has such a great, irreverent sense of humor. Perhaps best known today for having played the bitchy Alexis Carrington in the hit show *Dynasty* back in the eighties, she is happily married to Percy Gibson, and they are among our best friends.

I return to David Gest, who had by now been divorced from Liza after the "wedding to end all weddings" recounted in these pages. He had moved to Hawaii for some reason, claiming both mental and physical cruelty from Liza—totally absurd! He was now living in London doing what he did best, producing a big charity "do."

He called one day to invite us to attend this old Hollywood-themed event in the spirit of the wonderful ones he had done for the Motion Picture Home in Los Angeles years before, when we had first met him. This time, the charity was Caudwell Children in London. It was all expenses paid, with every studio star still alive. Why not? It sounded like fun. Our friends Jane Powell and Dickie Moore, TCM host Robert Osborne, and Sally Ann Howes and her husband Douglas Rae were also among the guests.

One day, a few weeks before our departure, David called to go over some of the details. He asked if I could think of any star he had forgotten. Why not ask Joan Collins? When Arlene attended her wedding to Percy the year before, we were so pleased to read in the London papers how beloved she was. "Our Joanie," they affectionately called her. David became pouty and said, "She doesn't like me."

"I'm sure she does," I said with my fingers crossed. "This is business, David. She is a big deal in London, and she is already there."

He begrudgingly agreed to think about her. The next thing I knew, Percy called to say they had been invited and thanked me. It seemed, I later found out, that when David passed the idea to John Caudwell, the founder of Caudwell Children, he loved it. It seemed he was a big fan.

As usual, the event was an MGM special, with Whitney Houston, in her prime, performing. As I said, every star of that generation was there, from Jane Russell and Carroll Baker to Lizabeth Scott and Mickey Rooney. After dinner, Caudwell, a good-looking and charming host, led a live auction with wonderful items. He had asked Joan if he could sell "Lunch with Joan Collins" as a special offering. Well, it was bedlam, with bidding going up to £250.

That's a lot of fans. Wow! I felt that I had done a good deed by suggesting her, but more so I was so amused that David, who had implied she was a "has-been" when I first mentioned her, now had to eat humble pie. I left the table to go to the "gents," as they say in England, and found our boy washing his hands.

"Still sorry you asked Joan?" I couldn't resist!

MGM Shoulders—
Jane Powell, Gloria DeHaven, Arlene

MGM's film musical star Jane Powell was an old friend of Arlene's. Jane's wonderful husband, Dickie Moore, was the famous *Our Gang* child star. They were two of our closest friends. Our columnist pal Rex Reed had told us that Gloria DeHaven, another MGM alum, had moved to New York. Arlene had made two films that Gloria appeared in, and we assumed she and Jane were studio chums. We invited them all for dinner at Doubles, the private club we belong to.

Jane and Dick arrived first at the appointed time. After having drinks in the lounge for forty minutes, we decided to go on to dinner and wait for there for our tardy guests. Maybe they were caught in traffic, I thought. I called Rex but only got his answering machine, and I didn't have Gloria's number with me. I told Jane that we had invited Gloria, thinking she would say, "Great, she is an old pal from Metro." To my surprise, she said, "Oh, I don't know her."

Finally they arrived, by now an hour late. Rex was perspiring and seemed exhausted. He looked at me and his eyes rolled. He later told me that when he arrived on time to collect Gloria, she was beside herself, having changed her clothes four times. He told her how pretty she looked. She proceeded to burst into tears, sobbing that Arlene was so beautiful and chic and Jane so great-looking that she wanted to look her best but felt a mess. Rex assured her we were all great friends and were looking forward to seeing her—not to worry.

They sat down, ordered drinks, and everything was going beautifully. I breathed a sigh of relief. Gloria, who looked wonderful in spite of her concerns, would preface her thoughts with "I know that I look much older than both of you girls, but I don't sleep very well and have issues with my breathing." Or "I know that I should exercise, but I am alone and don't like going to a gym by myself. You gals must have lots of friends that you can go with."

Jane, who does not suffer fools, finally said, "Gloria, I go by myself to class every Tuesday and Thursday morning at 9:00 a.m., why don't you join me?"

Gloria would say, "Arlene, you have such flawless skin, I am all wrinkled and blotchy."

Arlene would answer, "Gloria, you are so lovely, you look wonderful."

Gloria always saw the glass half empty, while the others saw it half full. Finally, during desert, Gloria got up, presumably to use the ladies' room. We noticed after some time that she was gone for too long. Jane volunteered to see what was happening. After fifteen minutes neither of them had appeared. It was Arlene's turn to exit to see what the hell was going on. The three of us guys couldn't imagine what had happened but agreed that Gloria was a handful.

After ten minutes Arlene finally returned to say that Gloria was dissolved in tears, inconsolable. Jane was helping her get it together to return to the table. Gloria, a great-looking gal with a good figure

Arlene Dahl, Gloria DeHaven, Marc Rosen

and a great personality, seemingly had such low self-esteem that she had convinced herself that no one liked her. We all felt terrible, but in examining the course of conversation over dinner, we realized that we had been nothing but supportive and generous in our comments. That evening, I learned an important lesson in passive-aggressive behavior!

Oscar's Shoulders—
Bette Davis, Tom Hanks

For many years, Arlene and I attended the Academy Awards and the Governors Ball (before there was a *Vanity Fair* party). We would always go with our friend, gossip columnist Shirley Eder and her husband, Edward. It was still a glamorous time when the Academy respected the stars of Arlene's generation and the idea of the host taking selfies or serving pizza was unheard of.

At one of these ceremonies, as they all seem to blur into one, Bette Davis, very old at the time, walked out alone, a huge error in judgment by the producers, to present the final, most important award for Best Picture. You could feel her discomfort and sat there praying she would get through it. Sadly this was not to be. The teleprompter was going faster than she could read. Too vain to wear glasses, she struggled to announce the contenders, much less the winner. The audience was very uncomfortable, aware this was being broadcast globally to millions of viewers and that there was nothing they could do to help. Ms. Davis was becoming more and more agitated, but finally and awkwardly got through it.

It was embarrassing to say the least for this great star. Everyone felt so bad for her. It was all anyone could speak of as we exited the auditorium and made our way to the ball. When the four of us reached our table, Tom Hanks, a terrific young actor who had recently starred in the film *Big*, and his fiancée, Rita Wilson, were at the table, but there were three empty seats. For a while it seemed no one was coming to fill them, until suddenly Bette walked in with her two guests and sat down. Clearly not a happy camper, she said hello to no one. Tom and Rita were dancing when Bette arrived, and we decided to join them on the dance floor, as Bette needed space to calm down.

When the music stopped, we walked back toward the table with Tom and Rita. As we got closer, Tom noticed that Bette had sat in his seat. In his best Big Bad Wolf voice he parodied, "Look who's sitting in my seat." He was not pleased. "I am going to tell her to move."

Looking him straight in the eye, I said, "I do not think that is a good idea. This lady is very unhappy. On a good day she is very difficult, but at this moment, I can't imagine her wrath."

He looked at me, and then it registered: "Good idea."

We quietly joined the table when Shirley Eder, fresh from working the room to get quotes for her column, said hello to Bette, as did Arlene. Bette of the bulging eyes made no response. Shirley, who couldn't leave it alone, said, "Bette, Arlene Dahl just said hello to you."

Everyone drew a breath as Davis stared menacingly at Shirley and said, "Who appointed you hostess of this table?"

I felt as if we were in a remake of *All About Eve*.

CHAPTER SIX

GRANDES DAMES

Technicolor Shoulders—
Arlene Dahl

One day, when I was just twenty-six, my friend, marketing maven Dorothy Friedman, called to ask if I would be interested in moon-lighting on a project that was independent of Revlon, where I was working as a packaging designer. My first wife, Rosemary, and I were restoring an old house, so I eagerly said yes. Dorothy was involved in a project to create a fragrance for the movie star Arlene Dahl. At that time, well before the era of celebrity fragrances, such an idea was unique.

Dorothy arranged for me to come to her office to meet Miss Dahl. I was only vaguely aware of who she was. I knew she was beau-tiful, had red hair and a beauty mark, but I had never seen any of her films. I quickly found out that she had been a big star at MGM. Louis B. Mayer famously said that she was "the girl for whom Technicolor was invented." When I saw her, I was bowled over.

Within ten minutes, she said to me, "I bet you're a Libra." I said that I was. Then she said, "I imagine that you were born on September 29th or 30th."

I was stunned. I was born on September 30th. I found out that Arlene was an astrologer and that she was incredibly intuitive. She told me that for her scent, Dahlia, she wanted something that was romantic and evocative of an antique cut-glass decanter. That is exactly what I gave her. The round bottle has a raised diamond pattern that suggests the petals of a dahlia blossom in an abstract way. It was glamorous and feminine, just like her. Arlene loved it. This was the beginning of what was to evolve into a beautiful friendship, a love affair, and, eventually, a marriage; we just celebrated our thirtieth anniversary. Astrology: I believe, I believe.

Sisters' Shoulders—
Olivia de Havilland, Joan Fontaine

Happy Birthday, Olivia

Olivia de Havilland, the great star of *Gone with the Wind*, *The Heiress*, and countless other classics, is a good friend whom we would see when we visited Paris, where she has lived for many years. On her eightieth birthday we happened to be traveling there and asked her to lunch to celebrate. We invited mutual friend Maggi Nolan, who had been the publisher of Celebrity Service and was a member of the Cercle Interallié, a beautiful private club. I asked her to make reservations there and order a birthday cake. The beautiful building was supposedly the former palace of a Russian grand duke.

We also invited Christopher Barker, actor Lex Barker's son, whom we considered our stepson, to join us. Christopher, in his early thirties, was well-educated, charming, and very handsome. From the moment we arrived, Olivia was taken with Chris, using her considerable charm to put him at ease. He did the same. Arlene, Maggi, and I were amused that, at eighty, Olivia was still flirting.

We had champagne in the lounge and went upstairs to the elegant dining room for a spirited lunch. Now it was time for the cake to be presented. As we were in the city where haute cuisine and patisserie were an art form, I expected a divine confection. To my horror, in came a green frosted sheet cake with candles avec a sauceboat of blue crème anglaise—a vile-looking combination. To

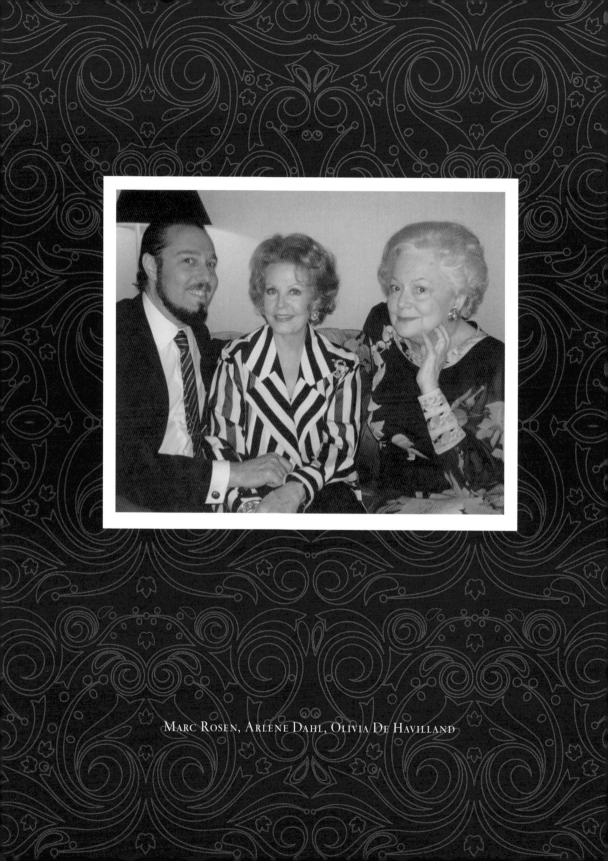

Marc Rosen, Arlene Dahl, Olivia De Havilland

complete the aesthetic, when the first slice was removed a chocolate cake was revealed within. The green and brown cake with the blue sauce set French cooking back by a century. A very jolly Olivia was oblivious to it, and in fact she had a second helping and asked if she could take home the remains. Sugar and a good-looking guy were their own reward.

Speaking of Olivia, there was for decades a famous feud between her and her equally famous sister actress, Joan Fontaine. Both Oscar winners, they had not spoken for over fifty years. Olivia's lovely daughter, Gisele, had never met her aunt.

Dinner with Joan Fontaine

Joan was very refined but a tough cookie. She was one of Arlene's earliest Hollywood friends, both being muses for Sir Charles Mendl, decorator Elsie de Wolfe's husband. Living in New York City, we would see her socially from time to time.

One night at a dinner party, Joan sat across from me at a long, narrow table. She had come with a "walker" who was seated at a different end of the table. We had a lot of fun, and after a vodka or three, she began flirting and occasionally holding my hand across the table. I played along, knowing she was being terribly chic and touchy and that it meant nothing. I had also seen her dark side and didn't want to do anything that would change her mood.

After dessert was served, her friend came over to see if she was ready to depart. She dismissed him with a wave and grandly said, "In a while, dear," and he went back to his seat. She was feeling no pain and regaling us with an amusing story. Most of the guests had left by now. He came back with his coat on and her wrap on his arm.

"I think it's time to go," he said.

Without turning around, she cut him dead. "Why don't you?" My blood ran cold. Those girls were salt and sugar.

Rebecca

Joan had been nominated for her first Oscar for the leading role in my all-time favorite film, Alfred Hitchcock's *Rebecca*, also starring Laurence Olivier.

Several years after that dinner party, Joan moved to Pebble Beach, California. Arlene and I had gone to New York's Paris Theatre to see the new Merchant Ivory film *Howards End*, which takes place in an enormous stone English country house. As we left the theater, we noticed Joan in the lobby. We embraced, and when we found out that she was alone, we invited her to join us for dinner.

At the table I remarked how much the mansion in the film reminded me of Manderley, the famous house in *Rebecca*. She agreed, and I asked what Manderley was like, assuming they had filmed in an actual house.

She said, "Oh, it was painted on glass."

Those art directors at the studios were so talented that they could actually paint a house on glass and light it from behind to create the impression of a real three-dimensional building. I was destroyed, my balloon burst. Manderley, the countryseat of the de Winter family, was a fake. Is nothing sacred?

SPLASHING SHOULDERS—
PATRICIA NEAL

Pat Neal was the loveliest person. Elegant, proper, and improper...
if you know what I mean. She was an old friend of Arlene's, having
had trysts with a married Gary Cooper at Arlene and Lex Barker's
house near the studio.

Our friends, Nancy and Gerry Tsai, who were married at the
time, had chartered a yacht and invited us on a cruise down the
New England coast. As we were stopping at Edgartown in Martha's
Vineyard, where Pat summered, Arlene called to ask if she would
like to come aboard the boat for drinks and then on to a neighbor-
ing yacht for dinner.

"That would be delightful," she said. "Can I bring a gentleman?"
Of course.

Recovering from a recent fall, Pat was using a cane. Since the
boats in the marina were moored on either side of a narrow walkway made of wooden slats, I was a bit concerned about her walking.
At the appointed hour, I glanced out from the aft deck and waved
to them from a distance. Pat seemed very chipper and waved. As
they approached our boat, her cane got caught between the slats
and she fell into the water between the yacht directly across from
us and the walkway.

She could have really hurt herself. We were shocked, of course.
One minute she was there and the next minute she was gone. In

the drink! Priorities first: as she had gone to a hairdresser for the occasion, even in her watery situation Pat was aware that she must keep her head above water at all costs. Not just to avoid drowning, but more importantly to keep her bouffant "do" intact. Just as we were desperately trying to figure out how to rescue her, a good-looking young sailor from the boat next to her dove into the water, pushed her ample rear end up, and put her in our waiting hands. Ever the actress, and without missing a beat, she smiled broadly and said, "Well, I hope I made a big splash for your friends."

Bouncing Shoulders—
Jane Powell

It was announced that the great Stephen Sondheim had written a new musical—it was to be his last—called *Bounce*, to be directed by his longtime collaborator, multi-Tony winner Hal Prince.

Was it about life on a trampoline? A bouncing ball or a bouncy personality? Not at all. It was about the dysfunctional relationship of famed early-twentieth-century Florida architect Addison Mizner, his charming but ne'er-do-well brother, and his manipulative mother.

Our friend Jane Powell was cast as the mother. Having been typecast as the "girl next door" during her successful career at MGM, Jane was delighted to appear against type as the domineering mother who clearly prefers and panders to the handsome brother Wilson—to the detriment of Addison, the talented, sensitive, overweight gay son.

Several of Jane's friends and family, including us, decided to support her by going to Chicago for the opening. Jane and her wonderful husband, child actor Dickie Moore, had been living there for six weeks of rehearsals. As Sondheim had not written a new show for some years, there was tremendous interest in *Bounce*.

Hal Prince, who had become the director du jour on Broadway for many years, was clearly "out to lunch" on this one. Jane tried her best, but in the first act's pivotal scenes that characterized the

ARLENE DAHL, JANE POWELL

mother/sons dynamic, she was directed to be her typical Jane Powell persona rather than Mama Rose. Even Sondheim's score was mediocre.

Dick had told us that Jane had the best song in the show, to come in act two. Well, it was a good song, and Jane did a great job, but Hal imagined her singing it in her deathbed amidst a heavenly dream sequence that included a chariot.

Oy! What to say to her at the after-party? "I wouldn't have missed it."

The *Chicago Tribune* review said, "*Bounce*...it didn't." I think that said it all.

Funny Shoulders—
Gunned Down by Joan Rivers

The untimely death of our friend Joan Rivers brought a flood of memories back to me. Over our long friendship, Arlene and I had been guests at her beautiful duplex apartment for breaking the Yom Kippur fast, Passover seders, and "just for" dinners." I had designed the packaging for her first QVC fragrance, Now & Forever. We were present at her daughter Melissa's amazing wedding, where the Gay Men's Chorus sang "Big Spender" as Joan walked down the aisle. She too was with us at our children's weddings, birthdays, et cetera.

We would have dinner every other month to catch up. One such evening, we met her at La Goulue, a popular French bistro. In those days in New York City, men always wore jackets and ties to dinner at restaurants. "Smart casual" had not yet happened. Most men have a favorite tie they wear for good luck or for special occasions. I have been loyal to Turnbull & Asser, a venerable British clothier, my entire adult life.

That night, I wore a new tie and shirt that I liked. We joined Joan at a table beside the bar. Arlene and Joan were seated on the banquette across from me. She had a large balloon-stemmed glass filled with red wine. She was gesticulating with her hands when suddenly, as if in slow motion, her wine glass fell over toward me. I instinctively moved my chair back from the table, but I was doomed. The red wine spilled all over my new tie, shirt, jacket, and slacks. Joan

Marc Rosen, Joan Rivers

was horrified but without missing a beat got up from the table, went up to the bar, pulled out the club soda gun on its long hose, and sprayed my tie, et al., with its contents.

"Club soda is the only thing that will keep it from staining," she barked as the entire restaurant witnessed the show.

"Thank you, Joan," I replied.

I then got up, hailed a cab, got to our apartment (just six blocks away), stripped, filled the sink with a case of club soda, put my shirt and tie in it, got dressed, hailed a cab, and joined them for dinner in ten minutes. The soda worked its magic, and the stain disappeared. Gunned down by Joan Rivers. What a great dame! In vino veritas! Some people are irreplaceable.

Wedded Shoulders—
Liza Minnelli, David Gest

As I mentioned earlier, we had known David Gest for years as an excellent producer of amazing yearly movie star charity events for Los Angeles's Motion Picture Home. He was very publicity-shy. Yes, really!

He had come to New York to produce an event at Madison Square Garden that included Liza, Michael Jackson, and more. Liza had been out of public view for almost a year, suffering from viral encephalitis and recuperating in Florida. Doctors feared she might never recover. Well, you can't keep Liza down. She came back to the city healthier but heavier and not looking her best. We had not seen David for some time, as he had stopped doing the Los Angeles charity event.

One night we saw him at a restaurant where we were having dinner. He came over to our table full of enthusiasm to tell us he had an amazing new girlfriend and wanted us to meet her. A surprise to be sure! He asked us to meet them the next night for dinner. I had heard a rumor that he was seeing Liza. We arrived at the small out-of-the-way Italian restaurant and, in a short while, in came the happy couple. Liza wore a gray fox boa with tails wrapped around her neck. This wouldn't have seemed odd, except it was summer. She was so pleased to see us, but she wasn't quite herself. David was beside himself, oozing charm.

"Doesn't Liza look wonderful? She is down to her weight in *Cabaret*," he proclaimed.

Hardly, but we smiled, trying not to make eye contact with each other.

The waiter brought a basket of rolls, and as Liza reached for one, he picked up the basket and gave it back to the waiter. Liza appeared not to react. He clearly had her on a diet and didn't care if we wanted bread or not.

The evening got progressively stranger, with David repeatedly telling us how fabulous and thin she was. Maybe he thought that if he said it enough it would come true. David, who did all of the talking, told us how they had met and how it was just kismet! Although the entire evening seemed peculiar, we told them how happy we were that they had found each other.

As we got up to leave and Liza swirled her fox boa around her shoulders, the tail fell off. I bent to retrieve it and handed it back to her. This was really a scene from *You Can't Take It with You*.

When we got in the cab, I said to Arlene, "This is a disaster. Liza will wise up and get rid of him." This proved not to be prophetic. We got a call from David the next morning to say that they'd become engaged that very night. Oy!

THE WEDDING

Well, now that it was official, we all hoped for the best. David was working wonders with Liza: she was looking great, and he was producing her comeback performance at the Beacon Theatre. It was a wow! She never sounded or looked better. They were the toast of the town, and even though David didn't seem like the ideal bridegroom, we all hoped we were wrong. His former shyness for publicity vanished, and he was more than happy to appear everywhere with Liza to lead the interviews.

David was kind enough to include us in everything. Knowing that Arlene was a member of the Marble Collegiate Church, the original home of Norman Vincent Peale, he asked her to speak with the new minister, Dr. Caliandro, to see if they could get married there. Caliandro agreed against his better judgment, never guessing the media circus that would ensue.

Way before the word *reality* was used to connote outrageous behavior on TV shows, this "reality wedding" was destined to be the benchmark against which all "train wreck," over-the-top nuptials would be judged. There were leaks to the press daily with details of the bridal party, the gown, the food, the celebrity guests, et cetera.

Can you imagine that the best man was Michael Jackson and the matron of honor Elizabeth Taylor? Bridesmaids included Gina Lollobrigida, Janet Leigh, Marisa Berenson, and Petula Clark, to name but a few.

If you weren't invited you would have killed yourself. The traffic and security were brutal. We got into our pew half an hour before the appointed time for the ceremony to begin. There were enough white flowers to fill Yankee Stadium. We were seated along with our pals Michael Feinstein and his partner, Terrence Flannery, as well as Joan Collins and her husband, Percy Gibson.

At the beginning we admired the flowers, people-watching. After half an hour we heard a rumor that Ms. Taylor, renowned for being late, had actually arrived only to discover that her stylist had left her evening slippers at the Carlyle, where they were staying. The wedding could not begin until they were fetched, as "la Liz" could not or would not walk onto the altar barefoot. We were on Eighteenth Street, and the Carlyle is on Seventy-Sixth Street—with traffic it could take an hour.

Bored and getting antsy, our little group threw all caution to the wind and had the best time dishing everyone. Gina Lollobrigida's black wig was askew. Hope Michael Jackson didn't forget his gloves. He would have to fly to Los Angeles to get them.

Looking around the church, literally every celebrity in the world seemed to be there. I offered that the only star missing was Shirley Temple. Arlene replied that she was probably waiting until Liza's next wedding.

The ceremony began with a flourish, and although everyone was wasted by this time, we all revived our energy to celebrate the infamous nuptials. The ceremony was joyous, but the kiss was unimaginably and embarrassingly long. Joan Collins aptly quipped, "It was like he was sucking the chrome off of a Cadillac's bumper."

MILLIONAIRE SHOULDERS—
DORIS LILLY

Back in the late eighties, when my stepdaughter, Carole, was in town on college breaks, we always invited her to join us at parties. Beautiful and great fun, Carole, a student at Georgetown, was always a favorite of our friends.

These were the days of "conspicuous consumption," when Donald and Ivana Trump appeared on the social scene. Virtually unknown, they soon became symbolic of the "Nouvelle Society."

One night, Carole joined us at a cocktail party given by *People* magazine publisher Dick Durrell, a childhood friend of Arlene's, in the glamorous penthouse of the Time-Life Building. Among the guests was Doris Lilly, a good friend, who was a great broad and the author of the book *How to Marry a Millionaire*. The title was famously used for a 1953 film staring Betty Grable, Lauren Bacall, and Marilyn Monroe. Oddly enough, Doris never married a millionaire or anyone else, for that matter.

Across the room, I noticed the Trumps. The Donald and his very blonde wife, Ivana, new to the New York café society scene, were working the room. Carole, Miss Personality, was charming everyone with her youthful exuberance.

Later in the evening, Doris came over to say she had just met Carole and to tell us what a looker she was.

"I told her, honey, if you want to marry a millionaire, let me introduce you to Donald Trump."

Carole was just eighteen and by no means looking.

"But Doris," I offered, "he is married and is here with his wife."

"Don't be silly," she said. "Don't you know that the best way to snag a millionaire is to steal one?"

Perhaps Miss Marla Maples read Doris's book, for shortly thereafter she did just that.

Rubbing Stritch's Shoulders

Elaine, or Stritch, as everyone referred to her, was our neighbor in the countryside, where we met. If ever there were two women who should have had nothing in common, it was Arlene and Elaine. Elaine was acerbic, tough, brittle, and so funny. Arlene was beautiful, feminine, soft, and charming. As it turned out, they loved each other. I guess opposites do attract. Arlene always said they should have played Neil Simon's *The Odd Couple* together on stage.

After she moved back to the city, Stritch would stay with us on weekends, alienating our housekeeper and drinking beaucoup Beaujolais, which she had me order for her by the case. You couldn't help but love her sense of humor, her stories, and her philosophy. In those days she chain-smoked as well. She eventually gave up both addictions, smoking and drinking, but didn't lose the personality that came with them.

In 1985, it was announced that Lincoln Center was presenting a "concert version" of *Follies*, Stephen Sondheim's fabulous Broadway musical. I had seen the original in 1971 when I was just out of college and never forgot the haunting visual effects and the wonderful iconic music.

Stritch was asked to sing "Broadway Baby," originally sung by Ethel Shutta (an original Follies showgirl) as the character Hattie Walker. It was part of an ensemble number. The big songs of the show were "Losing My Mind" and "I'm Still Here."

It was for two nights only and the first revival since the show's debut. She invited us to the opening, and we were to meet her for dinner afterwards. Although I knew she had been a big star on Broadway, I had never seen her on stage before—she was just our friend. Well was I knocked out, along with the entire audience. Elaine, the inimitable actress, had reimagined the song completely, making it an anthem to struggling actors desperate to make it on Broadway. She came out and literally stopped the show! I was dumbfounded. Our friend Elaine had stopped the show!

Afterwards, at dinner, I asked her what she was thinking during the ovation, which seemed to last for five minutes. I will never forget her response—an actor's response that impressed me more than I can say: "I listened to the ovation as if I were Hattie dreaming that she had made it and was basking in the imaginary applause."

There was nothing of "Well, I was thrilled, wasn't I terrific." Elaine was a true professional, and we loved her even though could also be totally impossible.

MORE STRITCH

Throughout our thirty-year friendship, Arlene and I always gathered Elaine and a varying group of friends to celebrate her birthday. We were in the audience as her guests on the opening night of her amazing, Tony Award–winning show *Elaine Stritch at Liberty*. At the end, she thanked a few friends who had enriched her life. She thanked Arlene and me for never forgetting to celebrate her Birthday (Groundhog Day). We were touched, we cried. Elaine was someone who could never express emotion in person, only in front of an audience.

ELAINE STRITCH, MARC ROSEN

MORE, MORE STRITCH

A well-known fact among Elaine's friends is how incredibly cheap she was. Born to a wealthy family from Bloomfield Hills, Michigan, a tony suburb of Detroit, and the widow of John Bay, the scion of the famous Chicago-based English muffin company, Elaine was very well off. She worked all of the time and never entertained, to say the least. When I once asked Gerry Schoenfeld, the head of Broadway's Shubert Organization, if he was bringing Elaine's *At Liberty* from the Public Theater to Broadway, he responded, "No, Elaine doesn't leave any change on the table."

When she died, she left an estate worth millions. In thirty years she had never picked up a check at a restaurant.

One day at dinner, to my shock, she asked if we had tried a new café across from the Carlyle Hotel, where she lived, called Sant Ambroeus. I said no, and she exclaimed that she would take us there for dinner. I was not holding my breath.

Sure enough, she called to set up a date. When the day arrived, she called to say she was rehearsing with our friend, entertainer Michael Feinstein, and had invited him to join us. Armed with my credit card, we joined them at the restaurant. Arlene and Elaine were seated on the banquette, with Michael and I across from them.

When the bill came, to my pleasant surprise, it was handed to Elaine. As she was looking down at it, Michael, ever the gentleman, lifted his arm to take it. I quietly put my hand on his arm and gently but firmly pushed it back in place. He looked at me like I was crazy. I couldn't make eye contact or I would have burst out laughing. Stritch did pay the bill. It only took thirty years.

More, More, More Stritch

One night a few years ago, just before Christmas, we invited her to dinner. I made reservations at the old Le Cirque in the Villard Houses. Elaine suggested that we meet at Broadway director Hal Prince's annual party and go from there. After rubbing shoulders with the theater crowd for an hour, I told "our girl" that it was time to go. She went into the kitchen, where they had prepared a huge buffet, and came out carrying two large shopping bags of hot food. "Elaine," I said, "we are going to Le Cirque. You can't take bags of food into a restaurant."

"Don't be silly," she replied. "I will just check them with my fur coat." Can you imagine the smell? Anyway, there it was.

At the table, she proclaimed that she had just shot up (she was diabetic) and that she would order a steak dinner to take home. She lived at the Carlyle Hotel in a single room with a small refrigerator the size of a shoe box. All I could think of was where she would store all of this food and how she could possibly consume it all. Then it hit me. Of course, she was tipping the hotel maids and bellhops with food. A lamb chop from Swifty's for the delivery boy. A chicken leg for the cleaning woman. She had it all figured out. "How'd you like a steak from Le Cirque?" she would exclaim to the desk clerk. That was "our girl."

Very Special Shoulders—
Helen Hayes

Known as the "first lady of the American theater," Helen, an old friend of Arlene's, was our neighbor in the country. Pretty Penny, her beautiful Victorian home in Nyack, New York, was renowned.

When I first bought Treetops, our 1849 estate on the Hudson, we hosted a Victorian garden party to celebrate Helen's eightieth birthday as a fundraiser for the Tappan Zee Playhouse, which had burned down. Through the ensuing years she joined us at our house for our annual smorgasbord (Arlene is of Norwegian descent), Christmas parties, family christenings and weddings, et cetera. When she was ninety, she was a guest at our "Seven Year Itch" anniversary party at Doubles, the private club we belong to at the Sherry-Netherland hotel. To complement the theme, I had Chinese back scratchers—ivory for women and black for men—as favors.

Three years later I received a phone call from Helen one day at the office.

"Marc, dear, I can't seem to find my back scratcher. You know, the one you had at your party."

I had no idea what she was referring to until it dawned on me that she meant the favors from the "Seven Year Itch" party. Puzzled as to why Helen Hayes, the most famous and revered actress in America, should be searching at age ninety-two for a plastic back scratcher, I asked, "Helen, why do you want it?"

"Because I have an itch," she replied.

HELEN HAYES, MARC ROSEN

I drove over to Pretty Penny and gave her mine!

About a year later, Helen died at ninety-three. Nyack, New York, had been her home for over sixty years. A devout Catholic, she had donated the altar in her church, where the funeral was to be held. The pews were packed. It was by invitation only, last rites of the first lady of the American theater, plus the first citizen of Nyack. Among the guests were, of course, Helen's son, actor James MacArthur; his wife; and their six-year-old son, Jamie Jr. The local priest was having his thirty minutes of fame. It was a High Mass with no mention of Helen, the woman, the friend, the humanitarian, and the actress. I was feeling frustrated that this guy was only interested in getting her to heaven and forgetting her earthly existence.

But then Cardinal O'Connor ascended the altar, the supreme compliment, coming up from the city for Helen. O'Connor was eloquent and mentioned that as a young man he had seen a performance of Helen's most famous play, *Victoria Regina*. He told of her incredible performance and said he would never forget the thunderous applause at the curtain call. He then asked the little boy, Helen's grandson, to stand. All eyes turned to this small child standing alone in the high vaulted chapel. In one of life's great moments, he said, "This little boy will never experience the audience appreciation as I did that day, so I would like everyone in this church to applaud Helen Hayes." I am getting the same goose bumps just retelling this. The applause was deafening. What a fabulous and inspirational send-off to a great lady.

Carol Channing, Carla Fendi

Dolly's Shoulders—
Carol Channing

Over a decade after I had started at Elizabeth Arden, we were launching Fendi's first fragrance in Los Angeles with Nordstrom. Naturally I wanted an Italian-themed venue and was told about the Virginia Robinson Gardens. The house was too small for our party, but the huge Tuscan garden with its pool and pergola would be perfect. We were assured that it never rained in Los Angeles in September, so we were good to go.

The Fendis loved movie stars, so we made the evening a benefit for the Actors Fund, a popular cause. Arlene and I made sure there were many celebrities from the film community on the guest list. Television stars, too—Carroll O'Connor of *All in the Family* and Larry Hagman of *Dallas*. Their wives were the chairs of the event. To add to the Roman atmosphere, I rented lots of classical columns and statues from Twentieth Century Fox. I arranged to have actors dressed as gladiators and to float water lilies in the pool to make it look like a garden basin.

The arrangements were in good hands and I had no worries— until I arrived. The sky was overcast; it looked like rain.

"It never rains in September, don't worry," I was told. It was too late to rent a tent. I had to pray. Then I saw the pool; it was phosphorescent green. Algae. It looked poisonous.

"Don't worry, it won't be noticeable at night."

Well, they were right about that. But a bigger worry was that there were no guests. No one had replied to the invitation! Again, I was told not to worry—no one in Los Angeles bothered to RSVP, they would just show up. I organized a team that afternoon to call up everyone who had been invited so we could arrange the seating.

In the end, it didn't rain, the party was attended by all the glitterati, and the algae were undetectable. But there were some anxious moments. At each of the Fendi dinners, there was a tambola, Italian bingo, to win a fabulous prize: a summer ermine coat from Fendi. It was the coat featured in the fragrance ad. Arlene attended the party with me, wearing a gorgeous emerald green taffeta dress and seated at a table with Carol Channing, an old friend.

I told her, "Please don't draw a card in the tambola, because it would be embarrassing for me if you won."

At the end of the evening, it was time for the tambola. I had been pressed into service to call out the numbers and to announce the winner. When I read the winning number, I saw a hand shoot up and caught a glimpse of green. Arlene! "I am going to kill her," I thought, but in fact, it was for Carol, sitting next to her. Perfect, the huge star of Broadway's *Hello, Dolly!* She got up, put on the coat, carried on as only she could, and got us great press.

Finally, the party was over; it had been a huge success. I fell asleep completely exhausted. At 7:00 a.m. the phone rang.

"It's Carol. wooon the coat laaast night."

"Yes, I know, congratulations."

"Do you think I could exchange it for a white one? Pl—eez!"

Why is God punishing me, I thought, grasping for words. "I'm afraid not. It's worth fifty grand, Carol."

Talk about looking a gift horse in the mouth!

"I know, but I only wear white because of my complexion." Carol wore the heavy, brownish pancake makeup she wore onstage offstage.

"Carol," I groaned, "try changing the color of your foundation!"

Perfumed Shoulders—
Polly Bergen

Arlene and Polly had been acquaintances on the Hollywood party circuit. And though they had done a Warner Brothers film together, called *Kisses for My President*, they had practically no scenes together. Our friend Rex Reed was a very close friend of Polly's, and once she moved back to New York we began seeing a lot of her.

She was quite a gal and loaded with talent. Good-looking, smart, with a throaty voice, the product of years of chain smoking.

I liked her and her no-nonsense philosophy. She had been a very successful recording artist and nightclub singer and, after not performing for years, quit smoking and resumed her career by belting 'em out in clubs. Her debut at Feinstein's at Loews Regency in New York was a smash.

Polly was not just another pretty face. After clubs, television, films, and records, she went on to design and manufacture a shoe and fashion accessory line and got into the cosmetics business with a skin-care line called Oil of the Turtle. We really got each other and enjoyed celebrating birthdays and the like.

Unfortunately, the years of smoking had taken their toll on her circulation, and she became plagued with health problems. After earning a fortune, a bad marriage had drained her savings. She and her friend Jan were living in a lovely building that also contained

REX REED, POLLY BERGEN

my offices. She told us they would be moving to the country, where there was less stress and less expense.

One day the office bell rang, and when I opened the door, there stood Polly clutching a factice, a giant perfume bottle used by department stores for display in the cosmetics department.

She pushed the heavy bottle into my hands and said, "We are packing up, and I wanted you to have this."

"But Polly," I replied, "this is the Nina Ricci L'Air du Temps bottle. It is real Lalique and very valuable."

"I know, darling, but it's now yours. I have loved it for thirty years, but you are the only one I know who will appreciate it."

I kissed her and said that I would treasure it.

Polly died last year after a long illness. Although it stands among my own collection of perfume factices that I have designed, I value it most. Thank you, Polly.

Looking Over Your Shoulder—
Shirley Eder, Barbara Stanwyck

Shirley Eder was the Middle America Hedda Hopper. Back in her day she wrote a syndicated daily Hollywood gossip column for the *Detroit Free Press* and had both a radio and TV spot. She was just wonderful. A huge fan of movie stars, Shirley never wrote a negative word and wanted her stars to shine for us all. She was one of the handful of gossip columnists who could make a film a success in her cities. Joan Rivers used to say that "Shirley could give you Detroit." When Sinatra or Streisand played there, Shirley was the only columnist they would give interviews to. All the old Hollywood stars loved Shirley, and she loved them back.

Her two best friends were Ginger Rogers and Barbara Stanwyck, who happened to have the same birthday. Otherwise they had absolutely no similarities. Ginger, a devout Christian Scientist, was fun, feminine, and very, well, Ginger Rogers. Stanwyck, or Missy, her nickname, was smart, acerbic, and tough as nails. Shirley and I spoke several times a week, and she became my second mother.

She shared this great story, which is a favorite of mine: Shirley was in Los Angeles having dinner with Missy at Chasen's, the famous Hollywood restaurant. Sitting at the number-one banquette in the front room, Shirley was talking a mile a minute, as usual, while Stanwyck was working on her steak. A party of four came in,

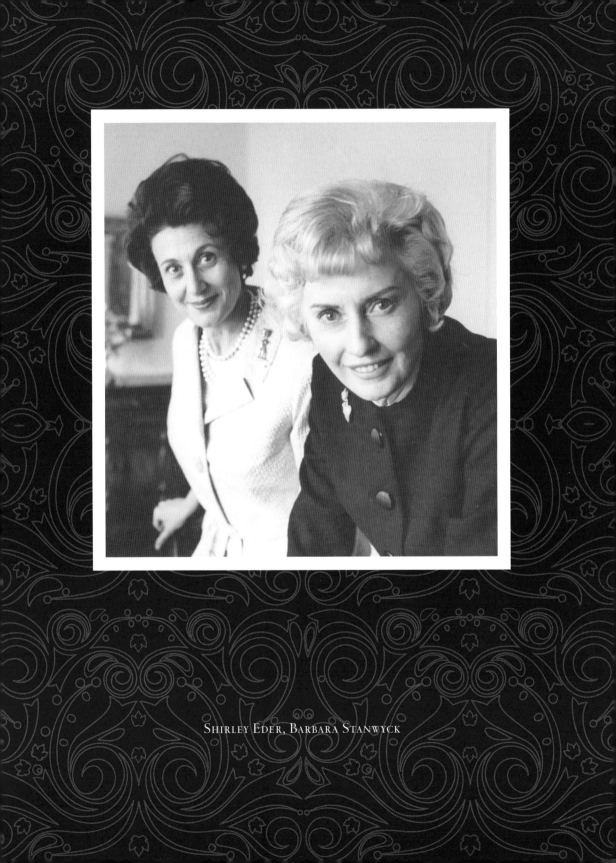

SHIRLEY EDER, BARBARA STANWYCK

spotted the girls, and made a beeline for their table. Stanwyck, who did not suffer fools, continued concentrating on her dinner.

"Oh, Miss Eder," they purred, "we are just in from Detroit and read your column every day."

Shirley basked in the moment but could feel Barbara stiffen up as the woman continued,

"Oh, Miss Eder, we know that Ms. Stanwyck is one of your best friends along with your other friend, Ginger Rogers."

Now it was Shirley's turn to go mum, as she knew that Barbara hated Ginger. There was a palpable pause as Stanwyck, continuing to look down at her plate and cut her steak, said, "Yeah, Shirley's friend Ginger Rogers, she doesn't drink and she doesn't smoke, but boy does she put out!"

Shirley wanted to die as her fans made a hasty retreat.

MARC ROSEN, JOAN COLLINS

Conclusion

Rubbing shoulders is what life is all about. It's all in "the mix." Life can be a smorgasbord of shoulders: of the famous, infamous, and just plain folks. I love them all. I have learned from them, and so can you. I have been a people watcher all my life. I love seeing how they comport themselves, dress, walk, talk, et cetera. I am open to conversation with strangers at a restaurant, in line at a supermarket, with a dinner companion at a fancy ball, or just catching up on the phone with an old friend. As a designer, I am tuned in to the details of how women accessorize their clothes, how men coordinate their shirts and ties, the pitch of people's voices, how they eat, et cetera.

Happenstance is a daily occurrence. Be open to it, recognize it, and savor it. You won't be disappointed.

ARLENE DAHL, MARC ROSEN

Acknowledgments

To Pamela Fiori for her support, friendship and for
suggesting the title for this book. I thank you.

To my Publisher Marta Hallet for believing in me
and for making this book a reality.

To Rona Shuster, my sister and personal editor.

To Stephen deAngelis, Peter Bacanovic, Sandra Leamon,
Terence Mack, Christopher Navratil, Natasha Nicholson,
Douglas Rae, Brian Reus, Donald Stannard,
Geoffrey Thomas, Liz Trovato, and Sudha d'Unienville.

Index

MARC ROSEN is a seven-time Fifi Award winner for his work in fashion and beauty packaging—an honor he shares with the likes of Tom Ford, Giorgio Armani, and Calvin Klein—and the author of *Glamour Icons* (Antique Collector's Club) as well as a professor at The Pratt Institute. His designs may be found in the permanent collections of the Museum of Modern Art in New York City and La Musée de la Mode in Paris, France. He lives in New York City and Rockland County, New York.

PAMELA FIORI is the former editor in chief of *Town & Country* and is a well-known writer and lecturer. She lives in New York City and East Hampton, New York.